To MJ,

May you always be blessed by a grander vision!

Best wishes,
Bill
July 2016

A Grander Vision

*Becoming God's Leader
in the Workplace*

By

Bill Cordivari

Copyright © 2006 by William D. Cordivari

All rights reserved. No part of this book shall be reproduced or transmitted in any form or by any means, electronic, mechanical, magnetic, photographic including photocopying, recording or by any information storage and retrieval system, without prior written permission of the publisher. No patent liability is assumed with respect to the use of the information contained herein. Although every precaution has been taken in the preparation of this book, the publisher and author assume no responsibility for errors or omissions. Neither is any liability assumed for damages resulting from the use of the information contained herein.

ISBN 0-7414-3355-9

Scripture taken from THE HOLY BIBLE, NEW INTERNATIONAL VERSION, Copyright© 1973, 1978, 1984 International Bible Society. Used by permission of Zondervan Bible Publishers.

Cover design by Jaclyn Cordivari.

Cover photography by Cyndee Cordivari.

Published by:

INFINITY
PUBLISHING.COM

1094 New DeHaven Street, Suite 100
West Conshohocken, PA 19428-2713
Info@buybooksontheweb.com
www.buybooksontheweb.com
Toll-free (877) BUY BOOK
Local Phone (610) 941-9999
Fax (610) 941-9959

Printed in the United States of America

Printed on Recycled Paper

Published August 2006

Dedicated

To Cyndee,
Loving Wife;
Joyous Partner in Life.

And the children:
William, Jaclyn, Matthew, Andrew, Raquel

CONTENTS

INTRODUCTION
The Journey Towards A Grander Vision i

CHAPTER 1
Roadmap for the Journey 1

CHAPTER 2
Personal Preparations 10

CHAPTER 3
Developing The Vision 34

CHAPTER 4
Focus On The Vision 55

CHAPTER 5
Energize Your Team 71

CHAPTER 6
Marshal Scarce Resources 90

CHAPTER 7
Execute The Vision 106

CHAPTER 8
Savor Victory; Learn from Defeat 122

CHAPTER 9
Become God's Leader in the Workplace 141

CHAPTER 10
Onwards and Upwards: Casting Grander Visions 153

Introduction

The Journey Towards A Grander Vision

Leadership is a gift from God. If you are a leader, you have been blessed with a special gift and you do not walk alone. You are in the partnership of the Almighty who created the heavens and the earth and whose timeline is eternal. This is the central premise of this book. I hope you will find this belief as energizing and as empowering as I do. Since this is the central premise of *A Grander Vision*, I want to share with you the pivotal events and experiences that shaped this point of view.

Reading the Bible

For most of my life, the Bible was an elegant-looking paperweight on the coffee table. The religion of my upbringing did not encourage Bible reading and, later, the language of King James was not readily understandable. I was given my first NIV Study Bible in 1990 by my dear sister-in-law, Helen Mayo. NIV stands for "New International Version" and it was a translation that combined scriptural integrity with contemporary writing style. As a "study Bible," it is fifty percent footnotes, explanations, and cross-references. All in all, it is very readable, educational, and inspiring. The Bible transformed my worldview and spurred a remarkable awakening in me. I was introduced, in effect, to the Owner's Manual of life, leadership, and vision. The Bible I would learn later is "The Word of God for the people of God." And our response to this incredible gift is, "Thanks be to God!"

Attending the Leadership Summits at Willow Creek

It was August 2000 when my senior pastor and mentor, Steve McConnell, invited me to attend a leadership summit of Christian pastors and lay leaders at Willow Creek Community Church in Barrington, Illinois. While I had recently celebrated my 50th birthday, this experience showed, yet, still, how small my mind was and how limited my thinking could be. Willow Creek Community Church is a big idea that started over 25 years ago in a movie theatre in the Chicago area. Today, it is a sprawling campus of a church located in Barrington that serves over 18,000 attendees each weekend and, amongst many ministries, conducts leadership training that is first-rate.

The senior pastor, founder, and visionary of "Willow" is Bill Hybels. I will expand on Willow within the book because it has and continues to be one of my most significant life experiences. But let me allude to just one of the many activities of Willow and, in this regard, I am referring to the annual Leadership Summit held every August. Approximately 7,000 Christian ministers and lay leaders convene onsite for a three-day workshop featuring prominent leaders from church and worldly leadership positions. Another 40,000 plus ministers and lay leaders participate by satellite hookup. It is inspiring, energizing, and educational.

In recent years, it has included national figures like Ken Blanchard, Chuck Colsen, Karen Hughes, and Randy Travis. One of the more controversial appearances was in 2000 when the surprise guest speaker was, then President, Bill Clinton in the midst of his impeachment challenge. Bill Hybels defended the decision on the grounds that this was a leadership summit and here was an individual who was a leader, professed a deep faith, and struggled with some significant human failings. Why wouldn't the President be an appropriate guest? It was a tense situation but a unique learning experience.

The leadership summit has noteworthy leaders from the secular and spiritual world. In my mind, it is a big deal and a first-rate event. It recharges my batteries. I come away every time as a better disciple, executive, and leader in every dimension of my life.

At the 2003 summit, Bill Hybels challenged the audience that their lives should reflect "a grander vision." Those words seared my soul and I have not been able to let go of them since. It was the moment that launched the inspiration for this book. I am immensely indebted to Bill Hybels for the transformational influence he and Willow have had on my life and my thinking as both a business and church leader. It has invigorated me to think big and even grand, and to make room for an inconceivably awesome God to intervene and provide outcomes I am incapable of.

Reflecting on my own journey
I will share with you within the covers of this book my personal leadership journey which, in a rough chronological order, would include positions in the military, politics, government, business, and church. There have been highs and lows; successes and failures. But by far, the most significant experience was learning that leadership could often be scary and exhausting when I went the road alone. But leadership became exhilarating, invigorating, and inspiring once I realized that I was in a partnership with God, and that my position was one of a junior partner in God's vast leadership enterprise.

Reading profiles and biographies of leaders from diverse walks of life
While there are not many leaders who make a big public deal about being God's partner in leadership, the more I read, the more I found that many leaders placed a significant trust in God to see them through their weighty responsibilities. One of my friends described it as God's "secret service." This subject needs more light and I attempt to cast some within the pages of *A Grander Vision*.

It also got me reflecting on my life in general. Specifically, I honed in on my journey as a leader in constant development. I could look back on all my achievements and, more importantly, the stumbles, setbacks and yes, lets call them for what they are...failures! It helped me see the Grander Vision of my Godly partnership and only at that point did I begin to accelerate, have fun, become more effective, and see the purpose and connection of God in my leadership roles.

I have been a participating student of leadership throughout my life and I attempt to share many of the mechanics of leadership preparation, development, and execution as well. Being in God's partnership does not mean you just sit back and watch or wait for things to happen. Leadership is a highly demanding role with rules to learn, skills to develop, and mindsets to nurture. I attempt to share as many of these as relevant. I thank the institutions of the Johnson and Johnson Corporation, the United States Army, Liberty Corner Church, and Willow Creek Community Church from which my most important leadership development has been gained. And I want to thank my parents for the loving, nurturing, encouraging family environment in which I grew up and allowed the leadership seed to flourish.

The purpose of this book is that you might see the Godly connection in your life as a leader, no matter how large or small your assignment, and to fully realize that you are God's partner. While I write this book primarily through the lens of my thirty plus years in business, I also write through the lens of my involvement of almost 15 years in our local church and the multiple leadership positions I have held there. As I wrote, I tried to continually think beyond my corporate experience and to process learnings also through the lens of entrepreneurial, non-profit, and faith-based institutions. I have aspired to make *A Grander Vision* applicable to leaders in these settings as well.

My ultimate intent in writing this book is that, after you have read it, you, too, will have a grander vision of your life and your leadership assignment in God's kingdom. And last but most importantly, my hope is that you will spread the word to the next generation of leaders.

Bill Cordivari

CHAPTER 1

Roadmap for the Journey

"Many are the plans in a man's heart, but it is the Lord's purpose that prevails."
- Proverbs 19:21

AWAKENING

For too many leaders I know, it is a major effort to get out of bed in the morning. They drag themselves off to a job that, long ago, lost any luster. It is strictly for the paycheck, their family, to cover their overextended personal finances, or the years left for vesting. In short, it is just a daily grind.

But there is no calling, little purpose, and absolutely zero vision other than to survive. The goals are to get through the day, pay the bills, and keep up a veneer of success for the neighbors. Please do not think I am being judgmental about others, for this is not my intent. The reality is that I am giving you certain slices of my own personal experience, supplemented by decades of discussions with peers.

But God has given us only one life to live here on earth. And he created us with several purposes to do something significant with our lives. The foremost purpose is to get to know him and all about him. If you do, one of the learnings will be that our work is important to God. In the first book of the Bible, God commissions man to work. After the fall, where Adam and Eve selfishly choose sin rather than obey God's commands, man is re-commissioned to work. But now, it is going to be extremely hard work. And, as will unfold within the chapters, it can be very stressful work if you choose to go it alone. And even more stressful if you are blessed by God to hold a leadership position and you attempt to go it alone.

The choices we face are living a life of drudgery or connecting with the Creator of the universe in a partnership. Leadership is a partnership with God and God is the senior partner! Please make special note of this point. Too often, people launch out with their own visions and goals and then ask God to conform and fit in with them. In the business world, one would get fired fairly soon with that kind of approach to the higher authorities. But the alternative is to pursue your gifted calling. Through prayer and focused intent, you can connect your current work to a grander vision of purpose and eternal connection. Or, you can plan how to maximize your current work for kingdom goals, but create a transition plan to move from pure work to pure calling.

PURSUING A LEADERSHIP PARTNERSHIP WITH GOD

A Grander Vision is largely from the perspective of my journey of course but I estimate about two hundred other leaders impacted the content. These are leaders that I personally interacted with over my career or observed them on the public stage and then read biographies and autobiographies about them. I have fully learned from scores of leaders in the Bible who accepted their partnership with God. And I cannot minimize the need and value for daily, continuous and effective prayer to connect with God and receive his messages and discernments about the grander vision for your life. From this core platform came most of my insights about the journey, the process and the disciplines required to transform your life from drudgery or lacking in purpose to one of crafting and pursuing a grander vision in your line of work.

I would like to share with you what I see as the thread of a grander vision running through my own life. To start with, I have been blessed by God with health, security, loving parents, and a large loving family that is an awesome gift and platform to build from. The word blessing can be misused in our secular society but I count health, security and family as blessings from above because I had nothing to do with them!

I grew up in the Philadelphia area for the first two decades of my life. As I graduated high school, I acted on an inner calling and decided to major in Premed and Biology at Villanova University. Biology is the study of the science of Life. I was permanently imbued at an early age with awe that life is sacred and has meaning and purpose. Where did this belief come from? I had an excellent undergraduate education at Annunciation BVM grade school (the BVM stands for Blessed Virgin Mary if you do not know the Catholic decode!) This was followed by four years at Cardinal O'Hara High School. So, while I was shaped by priests and nuns during my first eighteen years, I never remember one teacher saying, "Remember this: Life is sacred and you must find meaning." But I am sure it played a role. It certainly taught me the initial concepts of praying to an almighty God. I firmly believe that God is faithful to his followers no matter how broken, immature, or self-centered they are. And that description certainly fits me.

So, I entered college and pursued Biology, the study of life, for what I thought was a career choice: I was going to become a doctor. But looking back and with a much stronger spiritual platform to operate from later in my life, it is clear that I pursued Biology as a calling and that God had other plans. It was not going to be doctor. It was going to be pharmaceutical executive and leader in many other endeavors beyond.

I have enjoyed a career of thirty plus years in the pharmaceutical industry; a life-saving profession. In recent years, I moved from the world of large corporations to a small start-up company whose one and only product – i.e. focus – is to saves babies' lives. Saving lives. I think that is a worthy calling and a construct for living a grander vision. As a matter of fact, if you read through the four gospels that chronicle the ministries of Jesus, much of what he did was healing. He was a one-man healthcare company treating every condition known to man.

But I do not want to mislead you into thinking that I have had an effortless pursuit in the areas of God and faith. While I was harnessed into a lot of religious training and education by my parents up through high school, once I got to college, it was a different story. As a freshman in 1967, I was now liberating myself from my parents, the priests, and the nuns. I was now calling the shots and I did not need God. I had science as my new deity. I abandoned my faith and my connection to God for most of the next twenty years. Oh, I still had a relationship with God, but it was strictly to limit him to essentially two narrow categories. I will call them Santa Claus and 911. Santa Claus meaning that I still uttered a profession of faith when I needed something. And 911 meaning that I still called on God when I got into crisis. So, that was the shallow relationship I had between 1967 and 1987; Give me. Help me. Thank you God, I'll get back to you when I need YOU to do something for me. In between, I am not sure I believe in you or that you are all that relevant. I have science and I am going to become a doctor. I am going to make a lot of money and be respected by all. I am planning on a great life and I am not sure of your role, God. So, that is where I was with God a large portion of my life. I will share some of the painful consequences of this behavior in later chapters.

I am very happy to say that, in the late 1980's, I rediscovered my faith. It had been planted in me by my parents but abandoned by me when out on my own. My renewed faith and immersion in God's word just strengthened my belief in the value of a single life. The small voice inside me directed me to follow the call and pursue the path of a writer in the glorious tradition of Moses, David, Matthew, Mark, Luke, John, and Paul. I encourage you to be still, listen to the little voice, and take that first step in pursuit of your unique purpose and Grander Vision of your life.

Whatever path you feel called to follow, in the end, it is all about leadership. It is, at the very least, about leading yourself. One may be a corporate titan or military officer responsible for thousands of people; or a senior pastor with a staff of 25 and a flock of a 1000; or a solo writer who must engage editors, publishers, agents, printers, typists, graphic artists, lawyers, and others to pull a cohesive product together. Regardless of the size or scope of the endeavor, it is about personal leadership and about the skills required to lead others. Much of it is a learning process. This book is based on my leadership experiences in business, politics, the military, and in the local church.

But most of what I learned about leadership, I learned during my 22 years at Johnson and Johnson. I progressed through many positions in sales and marketing management, international and business development. My last ten years, I was in general management and became president of a $200 million business unit. I was, in essence, employed by an awesome leadership development institute. Most of the details of business leadership which I learned at Johnson and Johnson, I attempt to share in the middle of this book.

I have also had leadership experiences as a graduate of the U.S. Army Officer Training Program, as an elected township commissioner and as an elder in my local church. I borrow from these experiences as well.

So, how did I add writer to my leadership profile? (I mean if shaping people's thoughts and subsequent beliefs and behaviors isn't leadership, what is?) I have wanted to be a writer for as long as I can remember. There is a pen continuously connected to my right hand. I cannot stop writing notes, short letters to people, and journal entries. I have started at least ten manuscripts that have gone nowhere over the last 20 years.

Finally, one August night in 2003, I prayed to God something to the effect: "I think you have given me the gift of writing. I think you want me to write. I think it is connected to your bigger plan. But I do not seem to be going anywhere with it. If it is your will Lord, help me. Please."

During an ensuing two-week August vacation, my prayers were finally answered and I knocked out the initial manuscript for this book during that hiatus. I believe that I am on my way to the next level of God's grander vision for my life with a special gift he has given me. I hope and pray that I can share my learning with you and help you get to God's grander vision for your life.

HOW TO PURSUE A GRANDER VISION

You, too, can embark on a process of connecting with God and pursuing his plan for the grander vision of your life. The elements that I found essential in my walk included prayer, reflection, meditation, discernment, journaling, Bible study, and active participation in a local church as the basics. There were two more advanced elements. These are obedience to the voice of God and hard work. We will explore both of these tenets together.

OBEDIENCE TO THE VOICE OF GOD

I found it a long struggle and a lot of hard work to break away from the bonds of my own inner selfishness and all of the wrong messages the world and the media send me. Let me emphasize: it is hard work. But once you begin to discern or get to an inner understanding of the difference between the voice of God versus the other voices inside your head, you will have reached a momentous breakthrough. Who are these other voices? you may ask. They are the voices of the world, the evil spirit in the world, and your own selfish voice. These latter voices scream and God only whispers. So, it takes some hard work but I will lay out exercises to achieve progress and, hopefully, even a breakthrough here.

The reason this is so important is that, if you are going to accept the partnership with God, and if God is the senior partner, how are you going to get your directives and assignments if you cannot hear him? This is the first step of very hard and critical work. But the second part is even tougher. You need to obey every day. Once you hear and you have that confidence that it is God's will and voice for your life and your leadership, you must obey. Or else, you have little value on the team. The Senior Partner will have to go find another junior partner to carry out what was your unique assignment.

REFLECTION, PRAYER AND MEDITATION

I alluded earlier about the importance of a strong spiritual platform for "partnership leadership," which included, amongst several principles, prayer, reflection, and meditation. I found these difficult concepts to grasp initially but much easier with repeated practice – like most good habits! So, in the spirit of teaching you these principles throughout the course of this short book, I thought I would end each chapter with reflection, prayer, and meditation suggestions. My hope is that when you have finished *A Grander Vision*, you will be well on your way to mastering these concepts. Let me summarize the journey we are embarking upon and the roadmap that will get us there.

WHY A GRANDER VISION IS IMPORTANT

It is important because life and your role as a self-leader and leader of others is meant to be more than drudgery. God really did create you with a purpose. He really did give you the gift of leadership and, having done so, his intent was not to cut you adrift; to leave you alone as you struggle with immense challenges and opportunities. Finally, in the endless pursuit to become all that you can be, or in the classic terminology of Abraham Maslow, "self-actualization," I believe that this can only happen if you connect with and tap into the enormous potential of the Holy Spirit of the Almighty One. Then, and only then, will you self-actualize and become all of the unique you that God intended at your creation.

HOW WE WILL GET THERE TOGETHER

We will review real world experiences of how God plays the role of Senior Partner, whether your situation is good, bad, or extremely ugly. God is with you. We will go through the skills, behaviors, and mindsets necessary to pull off a grander vision. I will do all I personally can with the inspiration of the Senior Writer to convince and persuade you that you can live a life of a grander vision as a leader and that it is worthy of your pursuit, if you are open and eager to live out your calling.

Finally, I will end each chapter providing you with a platform to immerse yourself in reflection, prayer, and a meditation verse. The questions for reflection are intended to get you to stop the merry-go-round of life and breakthrough your own defense barriers and force you to confront important issues. The prayer is given as an example of real language that should be used in dialogue with the Senior Partner and to encourage you to relax, get out there, and then, get intense. The prayer is also designed to accomplish a couple of very important intentions. First, it is intended to model in words how to connect with the Creator of the Universe, Lord of the Impossible, and Senior Partner. That God would bless each chapter, facilitate your learning, and empower you to put the learning into action. Second, to give you some idea of how to make your prayers reflect the real world, day-to-day, nitty-gritty details of the leadership struggle and the answers, help, or inspiration you are seeking.

The meditation verses are chosen with a lot of thought and meant to help get you to an inspired endpoint of the chapter and the journey. With a meditation verse, it helps to stare at it, repeat it, write it, carry it around on a piece of paper. Write it in your personal diary, and connect it back to the chapter content, the questions you are reflecting on, and the prayers you are forming. Let's plunge ahead.

Questions For Reflection:

1. Do you have a grander vision for your life and/or your leadership, stirring around in your head or your heart or in some vague sense of your being?

2. In the totality of your life and your work, how much are you a leader and how much are you a follower? I am not talking title or business card or organizational rank. I am speaking of deep within yourself and dealing with the competing voices. How much are you a leader of God's intended principles or a follower of the world and the conventional wisdoms?

3. How much of your thinking is self-limiting and marked by excuses, denial, or rationalization to stay in your safe-zone and ignore the inner stirrings?

4. What really excites and energizes you at your core? If you knew 100% that you could not fail because the Lord of the Universe was empowering you, what do you feel pulled to pursue?

5. Where do you feel specially or uniquely gifted? Where do you feel that perhaps you have been called by God in a certain life direction?

Prayer

Dear God; almighty creator of all things as large as the universe and as small as me, help me know your grander vision for my life and as one of your leaders. I believe, Lord, that leadership is a partnership with you. You are the senior partner and I am the junior partner. Help me know what you have called me specifically to do and for what you have set me apart. I beseech you humbly in your Son's name. Amen.

Meditation Verse: Jeremiah 1:4-5
"Before I formed you in the womb I knew you, before you were born I set you apart."

CHAPTER 2

Personal Preparations

"And the voice of truth tells me a different story,
And the voice of truth says do not be afraid;
And the voice of truth says this is for my glory
So I will always listen... to the voice of truth."
                                    -Casting Crowns, *Voice of Truth*

GETTING CLEAR

It is not unusual for people up into their late 20s to muse upon the question: "What do I want to do with my life?" It is, of course, one of the most significant and often overpowering question to ponder. Of course, we deal with questions and choices all the time:

Red or white wine? Steak or fish? Mountains or seashore? These should be easy answers. They should be easy because, if at first you try and do not like the outcome, you can make a different choice next time. It really doesn't matter all that much because you get another chance to get it right tomorrow, next week, or next year.

But trying to decide what to do with your life, well, that is all together different. The stakes are huge, the clock is ticking, and we see these choices as ultimatums. We think they are do or die; no going back. And then there are so many conflicting voices and influences, all pulling us in different directions. Have you ever been there and experienced the inner or even outer tugs of: What do my parents want me to do? What does society expect me to do? What would my best friend think? Who am I really trying to please or impress? But the real question is, what does God want me to do with this unique and precious life he has given to me? We will tackle this question together in the succeeding chapters. It is most important, therefore, that we learn how to prepare spiritually, emotionally, mentally, and physically to take on all of these forces and voices and arrive at the place God has in mind.

We wrestle with the forces, the voices, and the inner demons and try to arrive at: What do I really think? What do I really want? We try to get clear. The answer should not be that hard. But it is and it buggers us often way beyond our late 20s. And it is all too easy to put these questions aside, like our income tax return or other painful tasks, and wait until the very last moment. But you and I need to clearly answer these questions as we sort our way to a grander vision.

I have wrestled with questions of this nature for longer than I care to remember. It is only in my maturity that I realized that it is not about 'what do I think' or 'what do I want,' but rather, towards what is God directing my life. What gifts and talents did God uniquely give me? Why? What does he expect me to do with them? It was not until my late 30s that I realized I needed to make room– a lot of room–for God in this monologue. After all, God made me and I believe with all my being that he made me with a purpose to serve him, his will, and his kingdom.

This seems like the appropriate time to clear something up and set realistic expectations. If you think there is only one roadmap and one journey and that we are all created to become missionaries to Africa or Antarctica, relax for a moment. The Bible tells us that the earth is the Lord's and all that is in it. You can be called to become the leader and a partner with God in a grander vision as a mother, a taxi driver, a hospital attendant, or a thousand different roles. I happened to be called as a biologist, business executive and writer, husband and father. I see a grander vision for my life in all of these roles but, for the scope of this book, most of the subject matter will be from my corporate experience as a business leader. The point I want to emphasize is to stay open to what the unique call(s) may be in your life.

I can imagine that, about now, you are thinking (or muttering) to yourself, "So, Bill, is hearing, listening, discerning and understanding God's will that easy?"

SHUTTING OUT THE CHATTER
Unfortunately, it is not that easy to hear or divine God's will. There are so many voices from the sidelines competing for your favor, that it is quite difficult to hear the one critical voice. It is not

your voice. It is your Creator's voice that is the most important. Unfortunately, He only speaks in a soft, loving voice with no force or pressure attached. While very difficult, it is possible to shut out all the sideline chatter. Then, there will be only one small voice and it will be clear.

I have been blessed to spend my entire career in the healthcare industry and the large majority of those years at Johnson and Johnson. I not only learned just about everything I know about business, but I learned so much about life and human development as well. I count this as a bonus and among my endless blessings that I spent most of my career at Johnson and Johnson; one of the world's most respected institutions.

An example of this "bonus" learning was a special occasion in 1989. Jim Burke, the CEO of J&J, was stepping down and passing the leadership baton to his successor, Ralph Larsen. The outgoing CEO had his last moment in the spotlight to say a few words. I will always remember the end of Mr. Burke's speech. He said that he was often asked, "What is the one thing you learned over your career that you might have done differently?" The room seemed to go completely quiet during the pause before his answer. He replied, "Always listen to the little voice inside. It will never lead you astray. Unfortunately, we often let too many years of our life go by before we understand this."

I do not know if Mr. Burke was personally referring to the Divine Creator. But his words ignited a spark that led me to that conclusion. At the time, I was just turning 40, and thought, "is that really the most important thing a CEO learned?" By the time I approached my 50th birthday, I found myself coming back to these words time and again. I could see the vast wisdom in them.

Listen to the small voice. Silence all the spectators on the sidelines. Hush all the critics writing reviews of your life, all the suggestions of people who do not really know who you are. Shut out the chatter.

Make room for God through the work of his Holy Spirit to guide you and lead you down his chosen path for your life.

BEING HONEST WITH YOURSELF

The summer entering my freshman year at Villanova, I had enrolled in engineering. I had a dull pain in my stomach for most of the prior month. Deciding upon a college major seemed like one of those momentous life decisions. But, fortunately, that August, I got clear and shut out the chatter; I did not want to be an engineer. I had no interest in engines or bridges or mathematics.

My Dad is an engineer. I guess I thought I could show him how much I loved him by becoming an engineer. But that was not me. I long dreamed of becoming a doctor. I switched my major to Biology/Pre-Med at the very last moment on the last day of the deadline in August for final registration.

SOLIDIFYING THE VISION AT YOUR CORE

I had a wonderful four years of studying Biology and graduated on time. My grades were something like 1.7, 2.2, 3.4, and 3.7. It was a slow start and a strong finish– but definitely not doctor material. College was a transformational life experience. I received a broad liberal arts education, rowed on the crew team four years, and had a lot of fun.

While I left college on a high, I was soon in the valley of despair after receiving endless rejections from medical schools. It became clear that I was not going to get into medical school with a 2.6 grade point average. I began to view myself as a failure (at age 22!) and my self-esteem and confidence was under attack.

Looking back, I can reconstruct my thinking as to why I thought I wanted to become a doctor. There were three reasons:
- make a lot of money
- be respected by people
- please my parents and grandparents who had already told the world that I was going to be a doctor!

With clear 20/20 hindsight, I can now see that these were all the wrong reasons for my having pursued the study of the biological sciences. But the little voice was directing. I was and am passionate to this day about biology– the study of Life. Little did I know then that, in the midst of my "failure," God was planting the seeds of a grander vision for my life. God was nudging me in the right direction– biology, but with his plan in mind. My plan was doctor, so I grabbed the rudder and steered in that direction. God's plan was biology, not doctor. Close, but not the same.

CONNECTING WITH THE HIGHER POWER

Today, I look back on the twenty years in the middle of my life living without thought of God's role in my life as the "wilderness years." While I broke off my relationship with God in college, he was still there in control of my life. And I give continuous thanks that he never let go of me or abandoned me during that time. I can now see in retrospect that, while God did not fit into my plans, I still fit into his. I firmly believe that it was the invisible hand of God directing me towards biology as a major and as a career pursuit. I firmly believe that God gives everyone special gifts and talents. I can clearly think of areas where God gave me absolutely no ability. Off the top of my head, the list would include singing, reading music, playing musical instruments, fixing things, anything mechanical or of an engineering nature, spontaneity, and the list goes on. But then, I can tick off the areas where he has given me special gifts and talents. These are areas that just come "naturally." My list would include: biology, writing, planning, analyzing, strategizing, organizing, leading, communicating, competing, debating. In short, God created me with a lot of the prerequisites to become a leader. He had a grander vision than doctor or biology major in mind and I now see it clearly. I give all the credit and glory back to God for any worldly success I have had. I now try to live connected to the power that is higher than me. Leadership is a partnership with God and God is the senior partner. I am the junior partner. I take my lead and direction from my senior partner just like any worldly organization does.

In addition to what all these connections have meant to my career, more importantly, they are the bedrock of my faith. My understanding of biology gives me strong insights that firm up my faith in a loving God and a power higher than me. I am in awe of the miracles of RNA, DNA, protein synthesis, and biochemical pathways. All of these complex reactions occur a millions times a second in a billion cells, day after day, with little effort on our part other than to eat, exercise, and rest well. I can come to no other conclusions except that, there, but for the grace of God, do I even take a breath each moment; that there is a loving God in control and that there is a vast purpose to life. Our spirit is housed by this marvelous, miraculous temple we call the human body.

FINDING THE OWNER'S MANUAL

The study and love for biology provided the first bedrock of my faith. The next layer of the foundation was coming to know and appreciate the Bible, the number one best-selling book of all times. Why is the Bible such a widely published and purchased book? True, it does add a very nice touch on a coffee table with red leather, gold plated paper, and colored ribbons hanging out.
But I think the real reason is because the Bible is the 1200 page "Owner's Manual" for life that God was loving enough to leave us as we were banished from the garden.

If you think that life is just work, toil, enjoy, cry, die, you could easily become confused and overwhelmed. Where is the purpose in all of this you might ask? Check the Owner's Manual. Everything you need to know is there.

CONTROLS AND DISCIPLINES

The book of Proverbs tells us, "Whoever loves discipline loves knowledge but he who hates correction is stupid." That may sound a little blunt to you but, obviously, God is serious about the point. If you truly desire to connect with your unique purpose from your Creator, it is going to take some work. It is not for the lazy. But nothing of significance in life is, so why should this come as a surprise? The Spirit will flow, but you must be personally prepared to accept the Spirit by developing life disciplines.

There are many life disciplines. I found the ones below most beneficial and as though I was unconsciously directed by an inner force to pursue them. For about the last twenty years, I have been fairly faithful to the following:

Pray often and continuously
Read and understand the Bible
Exercise regularly and stay fit
Eat and drink a high-energy diet

Read books voraciously
Be aware of the lies of this world
Learn the laws of money
Don't get attached to money
Build relationships around faith, family, and friends
Minimize alcohol and TV
Invest at least 50 hours per week in developing the skills and crafts of your purpose (60-80 hours is not uncommon)
Let go of the past. Don't live in the future. Savor the ever-present joy
Sleep what your body dictates. You cannot "burn the candle at both ends" without a meltdown sooner or later

I have discerned that these are the disciplines required for me to hear God's small voice, shut out the erroneous chatter, and pursue his grander visions for my life. Think about these and prayerfully ask yourself what disciplines are necessary in your life. Where can you build off some strongholds, and where do you just know you need to make some corrections and improvements?

LEAD THE WAY: You must lead yourself before you can lead others

I have made a career out of marketing and concluded long ago that, to be successful in marketing, you must know, watch, and understand the way people truly think. While most of my focus was on physicians and how they think about patient care; the role of a particular drug in the patient's overall treatment and so forth, I was also fortunate to have a stint in consumer marketing where the focus was: How do people choose a moisturizer? Why do people use such and such a shampoo? You have to learn their inner and deep convictions on the subject to have any success here. So, it would just be natural that I start watching and studying people about the deeper side of life. I recently chaired the strategic planning team at our church for the last four years. What does that have to do with anything? you may be asking. Just this: our focus was how to grow our church membership and spiritual vitality. To do this, we needed to understand how people think on these subjects. So, the team and I spent a lot of prayerful hours in this regard. From my collective corporate and church experiences over decades of human interaction, I have observed and concluded that most human beings are confused, unclear, undisciplined, and out of control. Most likely, so are you. I will confess to being in that state most of my life. While I have glimpses of glory and holding it all together through the grace of God, I continuously and chronically lapse back into this negative state because of my own innate broken inner self. I guess that I am proof positive of the existence of original sin in the human condition.

But here is the BIG point, so please do not miss it. Most people are anxious, worried, apprehensive, depressed, and, likely, so are you. Most people are weak, unfocused, and lacking in purpose and direction, and so are you. But what makes YOU different is that you confront all these limitations and demons head on. With personal will, choice, discipline, and the grace of God, you commit to rise above it. That is the big difference. You, as a leader, are as broken as your followers BUT you commit to rise above it. Small difference. Huge effort. Enormous outcome.

LEAD BY EXAMPLE

So, I think you are seeing the picture come into focus; that you must rise above all the inert brokenness, inertia, negative momentum, and gravity of this world that wants to suck you down. And, as a leader, there is one critical trait above all others that you must demonstrate. There are scores of leadership traits and behaviors: bearing, integrity, high standards, courage, judgment, flexibility, decision-making, work ethic, and scores more. The military had listed 26 key traits when I attended the U.S. Army Leadership Development School. A leading management consultant who served Johnson and Johnson for decades, concluded there were five critical traits. But just about all experts hold this one corollary as number one or right up there— you must lead by your personal example.

But above all – walk the talk and set the pace. The team will be motivated to follow your leadership by example.

LEADERSHIP IS CAUSAL; ALL ELSE EFFECT

You have likely heard it said that "it is lonely at the top." Of course it is. You are driving a higher personal and behavioral pattern than the masses. I recently had a conversation with a healthcare venture capitalist who, by published reports, has amassed a worldly fortune of close to a billion dollars. I don't know about you, but I was impressed by this achievement. We got to talking about leadership and he shared this vignette with me; he said this is what his father always told him: "Shoot for the top. Go after the number one slot. You know why? There is less competition there. Lots of folks want to compete for positions 2-10 in any organization but #1 is much more work and pressure. Few want to make this tough, lonely commitment." So, that was a long way of saying, yes, it is lonely at the top and that is why.

If you are an effective leader, your very capable team that you have hired or developed only delivers the unsolvable problems at your door. There is an impasse on your team. A major customer is ready to bolt. There has been a major schedule setback. You are running out of time and money. It all lands on your desk.

But you are the leader and you set the standard. If you run 50 mph, the team may run 49. If you run 30mph, the team may run 29. If you exhibit grace and patience, your team will learn from you. If you panic, scream, and make a fool of yourself, in time, you will have a team of screaming, panic-stricken fools. (The good people will have long ago left. The good are the first to go when they see a broken operation.)

But it does not have to be this lonely at the top. You can find solace in God and in his word. Remember the core premise: leadership is a partnership with God and God is the senior partner. It may not be easy but you will learn to trust in prayer, trust in God to equip you, and expect God to empower you. You will also come to realize that leadership is causal; all else effect. That means it is up to you. Well, not exactly. It is up to you, your God-given abilities and your trust in God to equip you with what you need to succeed.

And while it is critical that you get on your knees, or whatever it takes for you to truly connect with your Senior Partner, your leadership role is not a passive one. It is not, kick up and let God handle it all. No, it is apply yourself 101% to the fullest of all your God-given gifts, talents, and strengths and then expect the "Lord of The Impossible" to add the next 5000%! That is called Holy Spirit power, which we will explore later.

PERSONAL FITNESS

The importance of personal fitness on leadership effectiveness cannot be emphasized enough. Life is more than physical. We are Spiritual beings housed in a physical body for the physical world.

But our physical body carries the heart, mind, emotions, and soul. Therefore, our energy, stamina, the total hours we can work, the quality of our work, how we look, feel and act, is directly correlated to the extent of our physical and overall fitness.

THE LEADER SETS THE PACE

The leader setting the pace will determine the outcome. I was on the crew team in college. Our team competed in both four and eight-oar races. In either case, you sit with your back to the direction you are going. But you can see forward in the boat to the first person who is called the stroke. The stroke has to have leadership ability, good technique, and be in great shape. The stroke is usually the person with the best endurance. If they row 46 strokes per minute, so does the rest of the boat. When they settle to 36 strokes per minute, so does the rest of the boat.

As leader, you are like the stroke on the crew team. You set the pace across all the leadership fronts, such as work ethic, integrity, fairness, competitiveness, leadership, and grace under pressure. The leader sets the pace, which is adapted by the rest of the team, no matter what the endeavor.

PHYSICAL FITNESS

I have been at the physical fitness game for a long time. I call it a game because there is competition–you against gravity, time, and negative degenerative forces. There are rules to succeed or not. And there are winners and losers. So, trying to stay fit is just another game of life. I believe I got the physical fitness "bug" in college. I was on the crew team and we got up at 4:45AM to be rowing on the river by 5:30. And, then, upon graduation, I went right into an army basic training boot camp where we didn't start morning exercises until... heck... 5:30AM (I felt like I was sleeping in!). I have read all the books and dabbled with numerous programs. I have concluded from my own experience that there are four pillars of a successful physical fitness pursuit for me. You need to find what works for you so that you will be self-motivated to pursue and persist. My program consists of the following:

1. Aerobics – at least 30 minutes 3x/week. Run hard when you are young. Run intervals as you age and your joints get creaky. But RUN. There is nothing like it. Treadmill, eliptical, stairmaster, and Nordic track are all good variations when your bones cannot take the running anymore or just for the variety and cross-training of the workout.

2. Strength building – calisthenics, free weights, and weight machines. This is critical, particularly as you age, to counteract bone and muscle loss.

3. FUN– tennis, swimming, golf (walking, swinging, stretching). I also include long walks on country or mountain roads as part of the fun category. I find these walks synergistic in that they produce cardio effects, weight resistance to the legs, clear the mind, fill the lungs with fresh air, and allow me to talk and listen to God– all in one activity. (I will talk more about synergy later in the book.)

4. Nutritional discipline – If you eat good, you feel good and you do good. Conversely, if you eat bad, you feel bad, and you do bad...or badly...you struggle. You under-perform and are probably grouchy and sluggish, too.

I have read dozens of books on the above subject and tried to keep up with the science of fitness and nutrition. Also, on any subject, there is nothing like getting expert advice and training, and so, it is with the subject of fitness. Recently, my wife, Cyndee, gave me a gift of a three month enrollment to train weekly with a personal trainer at her gym. I learned so much about the best scientific thinking on weight training, cardio, and nutrition. I regret that I did not pursue this long ago and it would have saved me a lot of trial and error time. I encourage you to consider this also.

I realize that many people who are reading this section on physical fitness are groaning and saying, "is it really worth it?" Personally, I can tell you it is. Anytime I have been tempted to just let myself go and throw myself into work 24/7, I feel awful after about a week. The results are sluggishness, clothes don't fit well, grumpiness, and my energy wanes throughout the day. Yet, when I stay on my program, I feel high energy, good spirits, more productive, higher self-esteem and confidence. In short, I am in the zone to pursue a grander vision of life.

Here are some last points on physical fitness: Don't get too carried away in this area. Ultimately, the body is the "Temple of the Holy Spirit," a secondary shell for the superior spirit. It is a temporary vessel for an eternal component. But, on the other hand, you cannot ignore your body's requirements. I heard a fitness trainer say recently, "If you don't take care of your body, where are you going to live?" Think about it!

I know several chief executives of large corporations. They have reached the pinnacle of competitive worldly success and amassed fortunes that few could ever achieve. But at what price? They are physical wrecks, overweight, and out of shape. In their fifties, they now have back problems, knee replacements, and coronary bypasses as the outcome. Will they live very long to enjoy their fortunes, I wonder? Will they have the years to move on beyond business and progress to the transformational stage of deploying their leadership gift?

MENTAL FITNESS

I have covered a lot about physical fitness and, as I was writing it, made me ponder why. I think it is much easier to write about physical fitness than it is mental, emotional, or spiritual because the physical world is so measurable. Your fitness can be measured by a tape around your body, the scale, blood pressure cuffs, blood tests and so on. You can measure how far you can run or how many callisthenic repetitions you can do. But how do you measure the mental, emotional, and spiritual dimensions of your fitness. Let's explore and find out and come to some practical conclusions.

If it is the case with your body that you are what you eat, then for your mind, you are what you read, what you see, who you interact with, and how you process all these inputs. Essentially, what comes out of your mind is a function of what goes into your mind.

The broad selection of choice as to what you can put into your mind includes what we could broadly call information. Information can come from books, newspapers, magazines, television, radio, and online information for starters. I confess to being partial to books. I like the fact that there is a long drawn-out peer review or third-party quality control process before a typical book reaches your eyes. I strongly encourage you to read voraciously, continuously, and broadly. Read your specialty 50%, but read laterally and every other area the rest of the time. Read about any subject that captures your curiosity, no matter how far it may appear not to be a part of your specialty.

For instance, you may be an engineer and you mainly get your mental juice from reading about high-performance engines. But you have a whim of an interest to read about the growing of roses, for instance. Go with the flow. Read it. It helps develop lateral thinking and the other side of your brain. Personally, I have always been slanted towards reading rational, logical, business, or self-developmental how-to books.

But since I have started digesting the Bible as mental food over the last 15 years, I feel like a whole new world has opened to me. And it is very different from the adjectives I used above. The Bible is poetic, lyrical, and emotional. It is parables and songs and letters and prophecies. Reading the Bible started as a whim. It has become a life priority and, in terms of mental fitness, I believe a pillar of any personal leadership development program. I will say more under emotional and spiritual development, but it is worthy of a major plug speaking of the mental side of preparation.

I used to spend a lot of time reading newspapers, magazines, and watching the news. I have cut back on all of them dramatically. Here is my critique of each: Newspapers really do not tell you much that is new that is important. I find the daily papers boring and repetitious. I can click on my browser in the morning and any truly earth-shattering news is captured right there in 4-5 bullets. Rarely do I care about more than the headlines or I can click on the brief Associated Press write-up. If I have six hours to kill on a coast to coast flight, I will read the Wall Street Journal or the New York Times cover to cover. Both are extremely well-written. The WSJ feeds my conservative bias and the NYT allows me to keep pace with the liberal spin and slant on current events. I try to keep an open mind that the truth is somewhere in between. If they both agree on a situation, I have a higher degree of confidence that this very well could be reality.

But as Steven Sample writes in *The Contrarian's Guide to Leadership*, one should practice "going gray"– and he is not referring to your hair. He proposes that, before you latch onto what you believe is the black and the white of the matter, and as you sort through all the inputs, facts, and factoids you are receiving, stay "gray." Stay in the gray zone of indetermination until (1) you have to act on that information or (2) there is an accumulation of evidence that points to a certain truth or reality of the matter. I find this great advice and hard to do, like any good habit, but very valuable. In short: do not jump to conclusions; do not make a decision until you have to; use the time to gather as many inputs as possible while you attempt to reach the truth of the matter.

When Jesus Christ was before Pontius Pilate; the ruling political authority of that day, they had a dialogue about truth. Jesus claimed to be the truth. Pilate, in what could be one of the coldest, most cynical lines ever spoken, replies to Jesus, "What is truth?" His point at the time being, truth is whatever the person with the sword says it is. Whoever had the most power, money, or military victories determined the truth 2000 years ago. Do you really think it has changed that much today? I have reached a point where I minimize time wasted on newspapers or popular magazines. It is 90% spin. Much is erroneous and your mental time could be better spent.

Force your mind to go clear at bedtime. It is difficult, but critical for mental fitness. It is also a great discipline to both start and end the day with some time in prayer and in the Bible. I have a small New Testament which works nicely for reading in bed. It is lightweight and easy to handle. Last thing before you close your eyes, thank God for the day and his blessings, forgiveness for your transgressions, grace for tomorrow, and a peaceful night sleep. You can also pray to the effect of "Dear God, speak to me while I am sleeping. Plant the thought, inspiration or solution in my mind and I will jump on it tomorrow as the junior partner. Thank you my Senior Partner. Amen."

EMOTIONAL FITNESS
Whatever your situation in life; whether you are single, married, divorced, separated or uncertain, there are critical aspects of emotional fitness which include:
- Have a heart of gratitude
- Resolve or drop all grudges; they are emotional cancers
- Make time for friends and family; they are treasures
- Laugh at yourself, laugh with others
- Sooner or later get to the point that… It's NOT about you.

For effective leadership, the significant aspects of emotional fitness are pursuing and developing all of the above so you arrive at a point of internal security, maturity, and a focus on serving others. You will trust in God to deliver you from all of the anxieties of leadership and to protect you from any unfair slings and arrows which, if not controlled, can lead to brooding, negativism, and even paranoia ("everybody is out to get me"). Everyone in leadership positions goes through this. It is easy to criticize and even attack the person on top.

If you want some great inspiration from the Bible, I suggest reading the leadership development stories of Moses in the Old Testament (see Book of Exodus) and King David in Psalms. Both Moses and David are my two personal favorites as leadership and junior partner role models. Read just a little about each of these figures and it will become evident that they had a grander vision of leadership and viewed God as their senior partner.

SPIRITUAL FITNESS

I have touched on many aspects of spirituality in discussing physical, mental, and emotional fitness, so you might be asking 'what more is there to say about spiritual fitness?' Great question, if that is what you were thinking. The point is that more and more physicians, psychologists, and pastors believe in the holistic approach to wellness and fitness. Your body, mind, heart, and soul are all interconnected and, would you not expect this if you assume there was the same Creator of all four? So, there are many aspects of spirituality in the physical, mental and emotional aspects:

Physical- the body is a Temple of The Holy Spirit

Mental- the mind is a receptacle for good and bad inputs spanning inspiration to desperation

Emotional- relationships are really connections of one human spirit to another human spirit when you get right down to it.

With this as background, we can further develop the concept of spiritual fitness. Primary elements include prayer, spending time in the Bible, reading other inspirational books and works by people of strong faith. Also, keeping a journal of where you are on your spiritual journey is a great habit and process. It accomplishes multiple things. First, I am a huge believer in that, if you can get your thoughts on paper, you have a greater chance of getting clarity of thinking. Second, sometimes I find my prayer life is blocked, fuzzy, or full of distractions. But getting it down on paper, short and sweet if time necessitates, helps break the "prayer block." Third, as someone who has kept spiritual and personal development journals for close to twenty years, I find it incredibly insightful as to where I have made great progress and where I have been, frankly, quite a slacker and backslider. The memory can be very selective (or just defective as time moves on!), so having a written record to refer to has great value.

In your quest for spiritual fitness, thank God for your wonderful life continuously. Explore fully what your creation means. Read the Bible, it is the story of life – where we came from, what to do while we are here, where we are going. It is one of God's most incredible gifts to us. You will see me frequently refer to the Bible as the Owner's Manual.

Read spiritual books by bona fide experts in the field– Billy Graham, Charles Stanley, Rick Warren, Bill Hybels, C.S. Lewis, and hundreds of others.

Pray often, daily, continuously with gratitude for help, for insights, and for forgiveness for your weakness and brokenness. If you are moving on all fronts with personal development, you have taken a significant step to be ready to accept an assignment in the realm of a grander vision.

IT'S ALL ABOUT ENERGY

The sum total of your physical, mental, emotional, and spiritual fitness equals your overall level of personal energy.

The more energy you have, the more you can focus on a key issue. Give excess energy away to others and increase your odds for succeeding.

It is not an accident that sloth (the opposite of high energy) is one of the seven deadly sins.

Leadership is causal. Leaders set the pace. Leaders need high energy. Plan, prepare, systematize, and practice discipline to achieve a high energy level.

HARNESSING PERSONAL ENERGY

The most vital resource is the limited quantity of personal energy the leader has to apportion. The leader sets the pace. The leader decides on the agenda. The leader decides where she will apportion her limited quantity of personal energy.

In my own life, observations, and conversations, I have found some of the best uses of the leader's energy is to clarify vision, refine strategies, hire eagles, set the high standards, establish the culture (what you stand for, how people interact and behave), and drive the BIG IDEA.

Other best uses: dreaming, creating new ideas, teaching lessons learned to the eagles on your team.

Also, the leader is the desk of last resort for solving the unsolvable problems that the rest of the team and organization is not capable of resolving. This defensive use of energy will consume as much time in reverse proportion to how effective the leader is in spending energy on all the positive uses above.

INCREASE THE AMOUNT OF YOUR ENERGY

How do you increase the amount of your energy? Over many years, I have found the following to be the best for me:

- Get enough sleep. Whatever it takes for you personally to wake up refreshed. I prefer 6 ½ hours– 10:30 p.m. to 5:00 a.m. My wife, Cyndee, is also a high-energy person and she needs eight hours. Figure out your optimal amount and work it into your planning and expectations. You cannot take shortcuts in this area for very long. Your body, as a biological machine, will start to sputter.

- Pray at bedtime and clear your accounts with God each night. Ask for help. Give up what you can't handle or is bugging you. Go to sleep with a clear head from the day. You can resume dealing with the unsolvable problems or the BIG IDEA tomorrow.

- Eat a minimal amount of calories. You don't need a lot unless you are a marathoner. There are formulas that will tell you how much you need to remain in a steady state. My nutritional need is 1900 calories a day– not as much as you think.

- Minimize junk food, alcohol, and desserts. I have finally realized the connection between what I eat and how I feel. Usually, I feel good, that is, energetic, optimistic, and positive. Sometimes I feel bad– sluggish, weary, and out of focus. Then I catch myself and say, "OK, what have you eaten so far today?" When I feel bad, the recitation is usually: four coffees, numerous "small" Danish pasties, cold cuts, chocolate chip cookies, two diet cokes. Yuk! I feel awful. That is what happens when I let the inertia of the day run my intake.

- Discipline your dietary intake. On the other hand, I normally run a disciplined diet of the day: cereal, milk, fruit for breakfast; tuna on pita or a Caesar chicken salad for lunch; two coffees maximum for the day; continuous water throughout the day; and a small portioned dinner.

- Drink water continuously. The body is 90% water. The body needs water to conduct its one million biochemical reactions each second. You can go a month without food. You can only go a week without water and you will die. Water intake offsets the water loss induced by caffeine and alcohol. I spent ten years in the field of dermatology and learned that good water intake is the first step to healthy skin. Your face is the first thing people see and the last thing they remember. Do they see a well-hydrated, internally moisturized face? Or do they see a dehydrated, sagging leathery face? You can determine the outcome. (Besides water intake, other principles for healthy skin are– avoid prolonged contact with the sun 10:00am-4:00pm; cover-up in the sun; use at least an SPF 15 sunscreen; get enough sleep; take internal and topical vitamins that promote healthy skin. If you look in the mirror and see a vibrant face, you feel vibrant. If you see tired and weary, you feel and reflect the same. If your followers look at you and see a vibrant energized face, it can lift them up. Conversely, if you look tired and weary all the time, they may think, "Is this what I aspire to?" (I don't think so.)

- Take vitamins and other supplements. If you reach the point where I am, let's call it...a "mature age," you do not need a lot of calories unless you significantly increase your exercise. Through trial and error, I figured out that I only need about 1900 calories a day. That is not a lot of margin of error to get all the nutrients and vitamins I need. One easy solution is to find a good, broad-range multi-vitamin. Ask your family doctor for direction on vitamins and supplements, which are critical for energy. There is a lot of good science and a lot of junk "internet science" on the subject. Get the facts from your doctor or a nutritionist. I still remember the experiments from college where we had multiple variants of Petrie dishes where we nourished them with permutations of protein, fat, carbohydrates and vitamins and moisture. The dishes with everything including the vitamins did better than dishes with everything without the vitamins. Like your momma said, "Take your vitamins."

o Only hang around people who have a positive, vibrant attitude. OK, admittedly, this is not 100% possible, but do it as much as you have control. We all know that life is tough, people are broken, work is hard, and on it goes. I do not need people around me who merely reinforce or point this out at every turn. I get energized by people who have an attitude of:
- Yes we can!
- I believe!
- Today is a beautiful gift!
- This is a great thing we are trying to do.
- Nothing and nobody is going to stop us
  - Or, in the words of St. Paul, "If God is for us, who can be against us."

DECREASE THE WASTE OF YOUR ENERGY

o Minimize the time you spend with reducers. Reducers are parasitic people who function as human leeches. They just suck your energy away. Obviously, it is necessary to interact. But consciously and intentionally minimize contact with them or the influence they have over you. One of the worst hires I ever made was a human leech. Every time he came into my office, which was daily, he had an agenda. And when he left the office, I had lost or given something up in the corporate equation of scarce political capital. It took me awhile to catch on; he was a very good leech. Finally, my team came to me in near revolt and I had to face into it. When it was obvious that he was not going to respond to my feedback and change, I had to remove him. Minimize your interaction with reducers just like you would avoid landmines on a journey.

- Minimize/eliminate time spent on TV/Newspapers. Most of the content is not new; it is old. It is the same refrain day in and day out: "OJ, OJ, OJ" one year; "Monica, Monica, Monica," another year; move to "Iraq, Iraq, Iraq." Rarely is there anything new. If so, you are not going to miss anything for long in this day and age of technology. Let the followers and average pursuers of the conventional wisdom spend 3 hours a day or more on TV while you are pursuing the grander vision of your life. Lastly, most TV is negative, depressing, morose, and emphasizing the dark side of life. Who needs this? Why add to your baggage of life?

- Take charge of cell phone and email drag. I know equally successful people of rank and responsibilities. Some are "addicted" to cell phones and email drag and others equally successful and responsible are not. It leads me to conclude that it is yet another choice in life. Let go and let God as the saying goes. And trust your staff and your team who you are supposed to be developing anyway. Or, you can choose to be a control freak, consumed by fear and paranoia that something bad is going to happen if you are not continuously connected. Or, you can choose to be a total egocentric egomaniac that thinks only good things can happen around you as long as you are personally making every decision and making all the calls and know everything at all times.

- If someone on your team cannot be taught or won't learn, you are wasting time and energy. Replace. As I just mentioned, you are supposed to be teaching, coaching, mentoring, and developing your team so that you are not glued to a cell phone or email hook-up and they are capable of carrying on in your physical absence of the moment. If they are incapable of learning, you need to move them into a responsibility they can handle or you need to move them out of the organization and out into the huge vast world where there is positively something else better suited to their unique make-up. I firmly believe that God created everyone suited to certain kinds of jobs. You can help people find those jobs that fit them.

- o Don't do anything that anybody else can do. Delegate. Assuming you have people on your team around you who can be taught and are growing, then DELEGATE and do not spend time doing anything that anybody else can do reasonably as well. Preserve your time for those tasks and functions that ONLY you can do and must do because they are higher order tasks. (The subject of delegation is covered in Chapter 6 - Marshall Scarce Resources.)

Follow these five suggestions and you will have come a long way in conserving your precious energy and decreasing the unforgivable waste of it.

MARSHALL YOUR PERSONAL ENERGY

The late management sage, Peter Drucker, believed that "the effective executive" should continuously ask of themselves, "Where can I contribute?"

Ask yourself where can you contribute your time and energy to make the maximum impact on driving results, deliverables, or outcomes that move you closer to the vision.

What projects should you attach yourself to? They should be vision and mission-critical projects. They should be super strategic activities so that everyone knows you are driving these projects or sponsoring them and you have high expectations for a successful outcome.

Let me clarify what I mean by 'you as the leader attaching yourself to the project.' It does not mean that you get consumed in the daily muck and mire. That is the job of the "Project Leader" who is accountable to you. As Sponsor, you ensure that the objective is clear, the urgency is obvious, and that the team is properly staffed. You put in place an orderly and prioritized process in pursuit of the objective. First and foremost, ensure that you have chosen an effective leader to head the team! You also schedule regular, highly visible, and pain-staking reviews to track progress. That is how you as leader attach yourself to a critical project without being dragged down by it.

What people can you best invest your time and energy? There is hardly any other activity more valuable than investing time in your "eagles." These are the high flyers, the people who learn fast, have high ambitions, and the courage to pursue them. You can rapidly off-load tasks to these people. This way, both you and they continue to rapidly progress up the learning curve and take on bigger and more vision-critical assignments.

GIVE GOD YOUR BEST TIME

Give God quality time not bone-weary time. As mentioned above, spending time with eagles is a top priority use of time. The only thing more important is spending quality time with God, your Creator and equipper; the One who called you for a special purpose. Pray, plead, talk, listen. Layout your real problems and concerns. But do it when you are 100% attentive and full of energy and engaged. Give God your quality time, not your bone-weary time. For me, this time slot is 5:00 a.m., when my physical energy and mental acuity are both at their highest points of the day.

Questions For Reflection:
1. Are you shutting out the sideline chatter in your life? Can you distinguish the small voice within versus all the noise competing for your attention? Find a still and quiet place and discern, what is the inner voice really saying to you?

2. Have you opened up the Owner's Manual to help find these answers? If not, why not? If the Bible, handed down by God through the ages to his inspired authors, is not your source of truth, what is?

3. Are you leading a disciplined life or is your style more of the contemporary culture of "whatever?" Reread some of the suggested disciplines from this chapter and write down

what are the disciplines you are pursuing to prepare you for leadership with a grander vision.

4. How are you doing on the four corners of fitness–physical, mental, emotional, and spiritual? Where do you have a good program and where do you need a plan, a program, and the pursuit of intentional outcomes?

5. How are you doing at creating, preserving, and marshalling your energy? Where do you need to make some additions or deletions in your daily habits to maximize your energy to deploy in pursuit of a grander vision?

Prayer

Dear Lord, I plead for your help and intercession as I launch into the challenging terrain of seeking preparations, disciplines, and fitness so that I may be worthy in your eyes to pursue a grander vision. May I never forget that you are the senior partner and I am the junior. Your will is my will. I long to become your kind of leader. Thank you, Lord, for your love and grandiosity. Life is big. May I live big in faith and not small in fear. Thank you from the bottom of my heart. Amen.

Meditation Verse: Psalm 106:4-5
"Remember me, O Lord when you show favor to your people; help me when you deliver them; that I may see the prosperity of your chosen ones, that I may rejoice in the gladness of your nation, that I may glory in your heritage."

CHAPTER 3

Developing The Vision

"Where there is no vision, the people perish."
   - Proverbs 29:18 (KJV)

CAST THE VISION

You probably would not think of leaving on a long trip without a map or an itinerary. Most people don't just jump into college; usually they have selected a major beforehand. You normally do not just wander out the door aimlessly each morning but rather have a rough plan and to-do list of what needs to get done for the day. The point I want to make is that most leaders and other highly effective people live by a habit of: start with the end in sight. (See Stephen Covey and *The 7 Habits of Highly Effective People*). They do this almost by second nature. The problem is that leadership requires rising well above the realms of common sense and second nature, and that one go far beyond the shorter term "ends in sight."

Leadership requires stepping back and seeing the bigger picture of the entire enterprise or undertaking of which you are involved. Failure to do so condemns you and your team to a sentence of endless busyness, activities, and daily energy drain as they pursue "goals and objectives" but without a larger scheme as the true objective. Grasping this thought is a prerequisite to ultimately reaching for a grander vision in your life and leadership.

VISION IS A BIG THING

There is an important lesson in the following passages but I want to get all the full disclosures on the table upfront so you can spend less time thinking about the inner motivations of the author and all of your energy on the lesson. The disclosures: I have voted republican in every election since 1976. I am a card-carrying conservative. I think George Herbert Walker Bush would have been a better role model for our citizenry than Bill Clinton. With that said, enough of the setup and onto the lesson.

BUSH 41 VS. CLINTON, 1991

"I'm not into the vision thing. I just handle what comes into the in-basket." So spoke President George Herbert Walker Bush in the heat of re-election in 1991. Or, at least that is what the media reported he said.

Since biblical times, it has been recorded, "Where there is no vision, the people perish." The people, the U.S. people, did not want to perish; they wanted to prosper. The other candidate, William Jefferson Clinton, had his vision taped to the bathroom mirror. It read, "It's the economy, stupid."

IDENTIFY A BURNING NEED REQUIRING ACTION

George Herbert Walker Bush was defeated. Bill Clinton recognized that the number one burning need of the American people in 1991 was a desire to get out of rising unemployment and lingering recession and to get the economy moving. He promised it in the campaigning and he delivered on it during his presidency. He focused much of his political capital during his first term to keeping the economy humming. He filled a burning need. He was elected and, subsequently, re-elected due to political focus and having a vision.

Later, President Clinton got caught up in the scandal of the young intern in the oval office, and then wasted most of his second term denying, defending, and deflecting attention from that issue. That was not "The economy, stupid." That was just plain stupid. And that is another story all together.

So, at this juncture, I have probably offended both Democrats and Republicans but I encourage you to see the broader lessons beyond the political framework. Whether you think that George Bush did have vision or if you think that Bill Clinton did not help the economy, the leadership lesson is still valid: vision is primary. Where there is no vision, there is no direction. Where there is no direction, team energy is dispersed and not optimized. Then chances for success become slim.

So, I am trying to build the case that being driven by a large vision is a critical success factor for a leader and leaders who have a lot at stake know this. The president of the United States has a lot at stake. But there are many other types of leaders who have a lot at stake. Whereas I spent the first twenty years of my professional career building businesses and thought that business leadership was the highest calling (I really did), I later came to see that there were many other leadership assignments that could be just as important, if not more so. One of these primary examples was developing a deep respect for pastors of a local church. I came to believe that business operated on the broader field of the world we live in; that the world we live in is a hopelessly inherently broken place; and that the local church is the hope of a broken world and pastors make or break the local church with their leadership and vision.

BUILD THE COMPELLING CASE FOR ACTION NOW

All effective leaders sooner or later come to know the importance of casting a grander vision but still may struggle with the "how." My personal blueprint for the how came from Reverend Andy Stanley. He is the senior pastor of North Point Community Church located near Alpharetta, Georgia. In his compelling book, *Visioneering*, he writes that there are the three major steps in casting a vision:

1. Identify a major problem and a burning **unmet need**
2. Offer a **compelling solution** to the problem or fill the need
3. Build the compelling case for why urgent action is needed **now**.

These are the three basic steps in vision casting.

Thinking back to the context of a presidential election, the candidate practicing "visioneering" would:
1. Identify as a burning need, such as: get the U.S. economy moving again and equate that in terms of jobs, financial security, and the promise of prosperity.
2. Offer a compelling vision of how to achieve this and stay "on message" with the help of skilled campaign advisors and staff.

3. At every opportunity, directly or indirectly state or imply that the people could not wait or waste four more years and that their vote on election day was critical and timely.

That is how these three principles played out in an event that is momentous in earthly terms; the election of a U.S. president, arguably the most powerful position on the planet.

But I have also seen how these principles can play out where the stakes are just as significant or greater. I have seen leaders use these principles to drive critical care healthcare businesses or establish worthy non-profit entities like the Epilepsy Foundation. And I have seen these used time and again to launch churches which have eternal timelines and are all about the grandest visions.

So, there are certain principles involved in casting a vision. There are also other principles that ensure that the vision takes root and flourishes in you; the vision caster.

CONNECT THE VISION TO A HIGHER POWER AND ALL THE WAY TO YOUR CORE

One of these principles is connecting the vision being planted in you to a higher power and all the way to the inner core of your unique being.

Peter and James were fishermen struggling with terrible weather, tattered nets, and small catches. They spent their days fishing for small catches like perch. Jesus called out to them and said in so many Aramaic words but with the following contemporary interpretation: "Hey guys, stop wasting your time on perch. They are such small fry. But I know you love fishing. Hey, follow me and I will make you fishers of people."

Their Vision became connected to a higher cause that resonated to their passions, their soul, and their core. I use this as a dramatic example from the Bible but the lesson is just as important and possible in your realm of leadership, too. I have been blessed to feel this connection in many leadership situations spanning the military, political, business, and church experiences.

As a young twenty-something platoon leader in the Army Reserve responsible for forty people, I connected the dots and felt we played a small but highly-significant role in the US Army's contribution to keeping the world a safer and freer place. The importance connected to my core. Many of my peers saw no purpose to what we did and considered our training and maneuvers mindless. But I did not. Back then, the seeds of perceiving a grander vision were being planted.

I did a short stint in politics when I was in my early thirties. Many people find politics boring, distasteful or irrelevant. I believed then and believe today that the American political experiment which has survived for over two hundred years is nothing less than a miracle. It is a work of Divine Providence and God's hand is all over the fortunes and failures of our country. As a member of a local political party and later elected to local office, I felt I was taking part in one of the grandest privileges that had ever come together on earth.

As I entered my forties, my business career was in full-swing and I was president of a two hundred million dollar pharmaceutical company. We mainly sold dermatological or skin care products. As time went on, it became obvious to me that many of my customers, board certified dermatologists who had spent half their lives going to school, had inferiority complexes. They had come to believe that what they did was not important– it was only the skin they were treating, not the heart or brain or inner organs.

But I believed what they were doing and what our company was doing was significant. If it wasn't, why were their waiting rooms always filled with paying customers? Their patients must have thought it was important. Additionally, when I read the Bible, it struck me of how much of Jesus' ministry was healing people of their physical ailments. Jesus was a one-man pharmaceutical company! And many of the ailments he healed were dermatological conditions. No, I saw a grander vision to what we were doing at the Ortho Dermatological company and it was the essence of my leadership drive.

It was in my forties when I started getting into full steam of supporting our local church as a leader in many dimensions. Using a formula that was effective in business, I just started volunteering for more and more responsibilities. Just say "yes" when people ask if anyone wants to volunteer. It is the fastest way to learn additional skills and knowledge. Over ensuing years, I taught Bible study; children's education and adult education, wrote a monthly Bible tract, volunteered for a leadership position in our capital campaign, and employed the fundraising skills I had developed in business.

I chaired our strategic planning and vision team for several years and was then nominated and elected to our church's Session; the overall governing body. I came to believe fully that one of the most important uses of my precious time given to me by my Creator was to give a large portion of that time back to build his Church on this earth. The stakes were eternal and the vision was grand– again!

So, I have attempted to impress upon you that, in my leadership experiences spanning the military, political, business, and church settings, I have always been driven by a connection to my Creator, and a grander vision that was rooted in my core being.

LAY OUT THE ACTIONS REQUIRED TO ACHIEVE THE VISION IN SIMPLE TERMS

People have short attention spans and they are bombarded by media sensations, which include television, radio, internet, computer, endless cell phone stimulation, and even talking dashboards with the latest blue tooth technology. Today, there is telecommunication overload, creating clutter and chatter, and a universal attention deficit. Whatever your walk of life or leadership endeavor, if you are trying to communicate and reach the inner psyche of another human being, you have a major challenge.

So, the first thing you have to figure out is: what is your message? Second, is it compelling? Third, how will you deliver it with impact? Either one large silver bullet like the equivalent of a 60-second Super Bowl advertisement, or the good old-fashioned way of "reach and frequency?" This implies who are you trying to reach and how often can you effectively reach them in a short period of time to penetrate their consciousness and break through the competing clutter forces.

But before launching off into the tactics of message creation and deliverance of it, let's go back to the corollaries of vision-casting. Remember, there were three steps. In essence, they were: 1) need; 2) solution; 3) urgency, as in identify a burning need, provide a compelling solution, and communicate why it needs to happen now!

I want to use an example from my local church in Liberty Corner, New Jersey. Situated in central New Jersey, it is one of the most prosperous locales on earth. There are an abundance of Fortune 500 headquarters within commuting distance of Liberty Corner and our congregation has a disproportionate share of executives, doctors, lawyers, consultants, and other high price professionals with advanced degrees. You might think this makes it easy to raise money but it is actually a double-edge sword. On one edge, there are a lot of people with a lot of resources. But, on the other edge, because of how they have come by the money and the type of high-performance, high-stress environments they operate in 24/7, they ask demanding questions (like their employers) when they are asked to part with their resources.

Several years back, our church was in the midst of a significant capital campaign attempting to raise $3 million, which the experts told us would be a mild stretch. We started to fall behind schedule. After a prolonged period of prayer and stress-filled crisis management meetings, we decided that the leadership and our senior pastor needed to dial up the volume and crispness of our vision-casting. Our three-part message:

1. The local church is the hope of a broken world
2. With this money, we will expand our capacity to serve the needs of more broken people
3. Why do we need to do this now? Remember when you were on the outside and you were welcomed in. Don't others deserve to have their lives saved and transformed now?

We got more than the $3 million. The congregation responded with $3.3 million. With that money, we built a large family life center that doubles as the site of our contemporary worship. It is a focal point for youth activities, community outreach, and worship on Sunday. The lessons learned were: you need to break through the competing clutter by staying on message and you have to practice highly-effective visioneering.

This formula and approach can work in building a business, a church, a political campaign, or a non-profit endeavor. Why does it work? Because it breaks through all the chatter, sizes up the problem, it packages the solution and connects in a personal way.

VISION DEMANDS A STRATEGY

From vision casting, we move down the cascade to strategy. People hate to make choices. They just do. They prefer to procrastinate, delay, and dither. Or, they opt to talk, meet, form a committee, seek expert opinion, or find the right consultant who they hope will have the magic answer. This behavior also manifests itself in the attempt to completely pacify all stakeholders 100%– which is impossible. It is also reflected in decisions where limited resources are spread across ten ideas, or points-of-view, as if one can cover all bets. But this is not strategy nor strength. This is weakness, capitulation, inability to decide and if carried to the extreme frankly irresponsibility.

Let me paint a picture using the mythical mountaintop as the desired endpoint. Strategy or strategic thinking concludes that we will follow this one path up the treacherous mountain to our golden vision at the peak. We will marshal all our resources behind this chosen plan of attack to arrive at our vision.

A path and a plan was chosen and resourced. Many alternatives were consciously and intentionally discarded. A tough choice was made. That is strategy.

STRATEGY IS AN OUTCOME OF SWOT ANALYSIS

Strategy is not an impulsive flavor of the month fad nor is it a whimsical ever-changing "shower thought" of the day type of thing either. It is a conscious deliberate intentional choice, which is based on thoughtful analysis to maximize your strengths and opportunities and minimize your weaknesses and threats. Ultimately, strategy is your ticket to vision achievement.

This assessment of strengths, weaknesses, opportunities, and threats is commonly referred to as a "SWOT Analysis." Conducting a SWOT analysis can be extremely helpful in determining your strategy. A SWOT analysis looks at the following:

Strengths– These are things you or your team are really good at. These are your core competencies. You should always build from strengths both as an individual and as a team builder or leader of a larger organization.

Weaknesses – These are things you are not so good at. These are obvious or glaring deficiencies in areas that are important for successful achievement of the vision. As an individual, you are what you are to a large extent, so it is usually futile to think you will launch a career or succeed at a venture that keys on your weaknesses. The best thing is to shore up a weakness so it doesn't hurt you but, again, put more time on exploiting strengths and opportunities. With an organization, you can always hire, fire, restructure or change directions to address weaknesses.

Opportunities – These are things within the realm of existing competencies that should be capitalized on. Again, you should always build from strength and next, look to capitalize on opportunities.

Threats – These are external issues which, if left unattended, could sink you. Threats can be present; right here and now, or could be foreboding hazards on tomorrow's horizon.

Once you grasp the concept of the SWOT Analysis, it should be used in assessing your own personal vision, goals, and objectives, and that of any organization of which you have some leadership responsibility. Let me give two examples to drive these points home.

Individual

Let's say, hypothetically, that you aspire to participate in athletics. You are 5'9" and 165 pounds. You want to play center linebacker on an NCAA football team. Being realistic, I do not think it is going to happen. Why? Because you will probably get crushed by a 300 pound linemen running at high speeds. But, if you are reasonably fast and committed at heart, you could make the track team, swimming team, or rowing team. That is a rough, personal SWOT Analysis; assessing your strengths and weaknesses and coming to a realistic plan for success.

Organization

Moving from the context of an individual to an organization, the principle is the same. Let's imagine that you aspire to become a world-class pharmaceutical research and development organization, but you are having trouble recruiting talent to a remote location like Scotts Bluff, Nebraska. Your location is a critical weakness. You need to either shift gears and focus on the market and commercialization side of the business, or you need to move to New Jersey or California, where there is a large talent pool of pharmaceutical researchers.

STRATEGY SETS THE COMPASS FOR FOCUS, COMMITMENT, AND MARSHALLING RESOURCES

Let's go back to the analogy of the mountain again to further develop the concept of strategy. If the goal is to reach the summit, are we going by land or by sea to get to the base of the mountain? Scaling the leeward or windward side of the mountain? Which direction; North, East, South, West?

All of these metaphors are relevant, whether your pursuit is big business, an entrepreneurial pursuit, a non-profit endeavor, a church, or your own unique, individual life.

You must be clear on the strategy, the choice, and the path you are intentionally deciding that you will pursue. There are a lot of key words about leadership and strategy in those earlier sentences, namely: choice, decision, intention. Think about those words. Then, you can be intentional about applying scarce resources and doing so in a way that you marshal, or amass, the resources to form strength against a weak point to obtain leverage and a multiplier effect. This is why strategy is so important.

For many years, I was chair of the Vision and Strategic Planning Team at our church. The purpose of the team was to discern God's vision for the future of our church and then, with the leading of the Holy Spirit, to figure out the strategy. Even though the organization was a church, and the ultimate mission and purposes of the church are– to the outside world– mystical, spiritual, eternal, the same principles apply. SWOT, strategy, choices, decisions, intention, are all just as relevant in the makings of a successful outcome.

It was the early 2002 timeframe when I had a breakthrough experience in this matter as it pertained to my work. My eyes were opened that I should be praying often and continuously about my work and the strategy and people decisions that I dealt with every day. The words of King David from Psalm 24 rang in my head, "The earth is the Lord's and all that is in it." I took that to mean an extremely inclusive "all," which included my job, work, people interactions at work, and direction of our company.

I thought that this thinking was particularly relevant in that in 2002, I had moved onto to a small critical care company, and we were involved in serving hospital based doctors and other healthcare practitioners who were dealing with life and death situations daily. This was a heavy burden on my mind. In many of these critical care situations, 50% of the patients die no matter what is done, so it was not far-fetched to think that our people and products might be one of the deciding factors for a life hanging by a thread. I started the habit of beginning each morning of specifically praying over our business, the doctors, and patients we serve and the unavoidable people issues internal to the business that are a key part of any day.

My main point that I hope you are getting is that, while SWOT and strategy can sound so "corporate," I firmly believe that there is a place for these somewhat sterile concepts in church building and, conversely, there is a place for God in business building.

STRATEGY IS THE UMBRELLA; TACTICS ARE SUBPOINTS

People often get confused by four terms– vision, mission, strategy, tactics. Here are simple distinctions to help clarify some concepts that are critical to become a highly effective visionary leader.

Mission	Mission is your unique purpose. Why you or your unit exists. What is the purpose of a Boeing 747? The purpose is to provide fast, safe, reliable travel. What is your personal mission or specific purpose?
Vision	Vision is the place at which you want to arrive. What is the vision of a typical airplane flight? It is a destination– a new and different place to arrive at. The vision of the pilot and airline of our Boeing 747 example above might be: Depart Newark at 7:00AM and arrive Los Angeles 10:30AM. Can you see the difference between Mission and Vision? There is a difference and most leaders I interact with don't get it. The difference helps you clarify your thinking. What is your vision? Where do you want to arrive?
Strategy	Strategy is the broad umbrella laying out the choices, decisions, and intention you are planning to pursue. Going back to the airplane/airline analogy, the strategy of Southwest Airlines was to provide no frills, clean, safe, lowest cost air travel to those cities underserved and where, therefore, they could create a competitive advantage. That is a strategy. What is your strategy? What choices will you make and not make?
Tactics	Tactics are the sub-points under the umbrella and are the major tasks, projects, or activities aligned with strategic intent. In the airline example, tactics might be: ▪ Focus on cities where the big guys aren't saturated and there will be less competition

- Treat employees like owners so they perform in a highly-motivated fashion
- Stay non-union for lower costs and a competitive pricing edge but treat your employees great so they are not motivated to pursue a union
- You must be on-time or nothing else really matters

In case you have not guessed, I have been a platinum frequent flyer most of my career. I spend a lot of time on airplanes and I think about the airline industry as well, even though I do not work in it. There is value to metaphors and analogies in learning and communicating strategy. There is also extreme value to studying strategy across a diverse swath of industries and non-business organizations.

I previously mentioned Peter Drucker, who has long been considered one of the top authors and consultants on the subject of management. He recently died at the age of 95. I have devoured most everything he ever wrote and I encourage you to do the same. But here is why I bring up the name of Peter Drucker. While business was his primary focus, his broad subject was management, and he wrote on every aspect of management with applications in the business world, but also the military and non-profit.

I read an article by Mr. Drucker a few years back in which he had high praise for the Salvation Army, a non-profit, as one of the best run organizations anywhere. And the main point I want to underscore is that he credited much of their success with the fact that they stayed true and consistent to their mission and vision over a long period of time. Determining strategy is an intense activity but it is secondary to staying true to your mission and vision.

STRATEGY IS YOUR TANGIBLE
TO THE INTANGIBLE VISION

Strategy also plays a key role in anchoring you as leader and your team on the right course and direction. Vision is usually nebulous by nature because, if it is truly challenging, then it is way out there- big, scary, looking impossible. It is what author and consultant, Jim Collins, refers to as "BHAGs"– big hairy audacious goals. Your team will continually say that they do not know what the vision is, even though you may tell them 5x/day. Some examples of an organizational vision and the key strategies from my business and church experiences may help clarify.

Business

Vision: To become a world class specialty pharmaceutical company, focused in critical care with sales tripling to half a billion dollars in five years.

Strategies

- Grow the existing core business
- Develop new product indications for core product
- License and acquire new products and/or small companies
- Geographically expand to rest of world outside of USA
- Continuously upgrade operational and organizational excellence

Church

Vision: To transform our world by becoming a Compelling Christ-centered Community. (A Compelling Christ-centered Community is a community of Christ's disciples whose lives together, centered upon the life-giving presence of Jesus and open to the power of the Holy Spirit, compel people to draw near to Christ.)

Strategies (Ministry priorities next five years)

- Evangelism- spread the word of the gospel of Jesus Christ
- Discipleship- live a life reflective of Jesus
- Excellence in Ministry- give God our best in all our ministries and programs; not our leftover efforts, energy, and resources
- Holistic Stewardship- develop a worldview that all you have was provided to you by God
- Mission- spread the gospel and our affluence beyond our shores and local community

The strategies and the aligned tactics and the corresponding projects, activities, and tasks keep people on the right path towards achievement of the vision day by day over a long period of time. But they can miss the forest, for the trees so continually explain and over-communicate how the strategy (here and now) connects to the Vision (way out there). Let's discuss a timeless approach for reinforcing and implanting all of this.

GET IT ALL DOWN IN WRITING
Thousands of years ago, as captured in the early pages of the Old Testament in the Bible, one of my leadership idols, Moses, has been appointed by God to be the leader of the Israelites. At one point in this drama, Moses is on the mountaintop in the presence of God when God gives him the Ten Commandments. And as he does, God instructs Moses, "Write this down." And Moses proceeds to carve out the Ten Commandments in stone, which was the technology of the day. The point is, Moses got it down in writing so that these ten strategies for living a Godly life, if you will, could become something of permanence. And, obviously, they did.

Most legal experts credit the Ten Commandments as the foundation for the legal system that evolved in the western world over thousands of years. The moral of the story is: get it down in writing!

I am a firm believer that, if you can't get what is in your head down on paper, chances are that you are really not clear on what you are trying to say and you vastly increase the challenges you face in communicating and executing against a vision, strategy, or tactic. I never cease to be amazed how people cannot get their idea, plan, resume, business proposal, or meeting objectives down on paper. When you ask them why not, they tell you it is in their heads. Then, when you ask them what exactly is in their heads, they cannot tell you.

I conclude that they cannot get it on paper because it is not straight in their heads. All people in senior positions of authority whom you may be dependent on for time, money, or other resources know this as well. Therefore, it is sad but realistic to say that your proposal is dead on arrival if you cannot clearly communicate key concepts like your resume, vision, mission, strategy, or a business plan in writing. This may sound a little rough to you but I have seen it and personally experienced it too many times. If the above hits home, then accept the feedback. Get to work and get it in writing!

PUTTING IT ON PAPER ALLOWS YOU TO PRUNE YOUR THOUGHTS, CONNECT THEM, TIGHTEN THEM.

The bigger your vision, the higher the complexity factor and the more moving parts there are. I realize that people are hard-wired in different ways, so what works for me may not work for you. But I have found one of the most critical success factors of my life in virtually all its dimensions is to get it down on paper. I find that continuous scribbling, doodling, bubbling, and linking on a writing pad allows me to work through problems, challenges, complexity, emotions, and finances– and, also, see the relations between all the moving pieces.

Sometimes when I feel overwhelmed and at a high stress level, I get it ALL down on paper and map out everything that is on my mind, on my plate, on my deadline calendar, and I discover a clearer reality of the situation. I uncover things like, I really don't have 50 things to do this week, it just feels like it. The reality may become clear that I only have five "do or die" tasks, I must accomplish 45 "nice to do if I have time left over" kind of things.

This works in my personal life and I also find that it works in my business leadership life. A staff member may tell me that he is overwhelmed with "stuff" and have more work than they can handle. I then ask them to meet with me to review the entire complete exhaustive list of stuff they are working on. Two things usually happen. One, I usually do not see them again for at least a week. It is either not that important or they just can't get it down on paper.

Once they get it all down on paper, we can have discussions about the values of certain tasks or projects. Does it connect back to the vision, the mission, and the primary strategies? I can help them prune the list, reprioritize, and take a good deal of stress out of their system. I have empowered my staff to ask "why?" If I give them an assignment or their boss gives them an assignment and it doesn't make sense to them, I want them to ask me or my staff "why?" Why are we doing this? Is it important? Does it drive vision, mission, strategic priorities? One of my younger up-and-coming staffers found this so liberating, he had the three letter word WHY blown up, laminated, and posted on his door for all to see. It became a point of humor but also a crystallizing totem.

As you are developing a vision, mission, and strategy for a venture or enterprise, get it all down on paper. You may discover that ten strategies really are not necessary and that only three are pivotal to success. Further, there are only ten critical projects or programs across them. Many should have interlinkage. That is just some of the power of this exercise. So remember what God said to Moses, "Write this down!" Back then it was stones. Today it is paper or personal computer. Regardless, write it down. Get it on paper. I cannot emphasize this enough.

CLARITY ON PAPER ALLOWS YOU TO COMMUNICATE UP, DOWN, AND SIDEWAYS

You will make your role as a vision-casting leader incredibly difficult if you cannot get important concepts and proposals down on paper. You need to be able to communicate up to your superiors and, ultimately, owners (in business) or sources of funding (non-profit or church) what it is you are trying to accomplish with THEIR funds. You need to communicate downwards to your team and staff and get them aligned. You need to rally the support of your peers who you turn towards for help, time, and resources. Regardless of the direction you are trying to lead– up, down, or sideways, you will have difficulty getting any traction if you cannot get your thoughts, plans, and proposal in clear and concise written format.

Your future employer, boss, bank, venture capitalist, financier, or approval committee has to have confidence and understanding before they commit to you. They want to see your comprehensive thinking in writing.

Your team needs something that is tangible, permanent, and clearly communicates. Words spoken evaporate in thin air. Judgments and confidence can be rendered on the written word.

Get clear in your head and then, get your thoughts down in writing. Organize, reorganize, edit, prune, and polish until you are beaming at your finished product. You have likely arrived at a state of clarity that you and others can rapidly comprehend.

WRITE THE ONE-PAGE GAME PLAN

I am personally hardwired for better or worse that if something is out of my sight, it is usually out of my mind. Out of sight equals out of mind. While there is a need and a place for a fifty-page strategic plan on top of twenty pages of budgets, I will comprehend the big picture but also get lost in the details. I need a summary document. For me, again, out of sight is out of mind. I need to have it all on one page that I can see at a glance. I need a comprehensive road map. I need a one-page game plan!

WHAT GOES ON THE ONE-PAGE GAME PLAN

The one-page game plan is a comprehensive document in multicolor with adequate white space and contains your mission, (purpose), vision (destination), strategy (intentional choice/path), and key tactics (major programs or projects). Also, put your budget/expenses up by tactics and key projects on the game plan. List your key metrics and milestones (goals and objectives) as well. Refer to the attachments for examples and a personal worksheet. I particularly like a lot of vibrant colors to energize the senses and make it easier to sear into the memory.

WHAT YOU DO WITH THE ONE-PAGE GAME PLAN

You, as the leader, should be able to unconsciously memorize the one-page game plan because it is emblazoned in your brain and psyche. You continuously prune it, update, revise, hone, and make mid-course corrections. You give it to all members of your team and communicate your expectations that they will align around it and, most importantly, own it. This is your long-range vision and short-term activity alignment mechanism. It is a compass and a road map. It is a tool for reinforcing vision and marshalling scarce resources most effectively.

THE POWER OF THE ONE-PAGE GAME PLAN

The one-page game plan allows you to get everybody above, below, and lateral "singing off the same page." And that page is your one-page game plan. No one can say, "I don't know here we are going." Look at the one-page game plan! You have eliminated distraction, diffusion, confusion. You have created a competitive advantage. You have created focus, power, leverage, synergy and taken a major step towards victory and achievement of your vision.

Questions For Reflection:

1. Do you have a clear discernment or vision of God's special purpose for your leadership?

2. Are you prepared to put in time and effort and prayer to achieve this state? Given the importance of the matter, if not, why not?

3. Strategy is about choices, crisp decisions, and intentionality. How are you doing in your personal leadership with this and how are you doing in your role within an organization, be it church, business, non-profit, or other?

4. Have you ever done a personal SWOT analysis as a leader? Do you have a clear understanding of your own strengths and weaknesses; the opportunities for explosive growth; the threats that might undermine you? Do this exercise first for yourself and then apply the process to your organization.

5. Do you grasp the power of the written word? Are you ready to commit to get your personal goals and objectives and that of your organization down on paper via the one-page game plan? If not, why not?

Prayer

Dear Lord, help me learn with clarity your vision for my personal leadership and that of the organization I serve as a leader. Help me be honest with myself about my SWOT. From this, give me the strength and the courage to pursue strategies that reflect crisp choices, decisiveness, and intentionality. Lastly, Lord, give me the patience, persistence, and the discipline to get it all down on paper so I can be more effective in my leadership. I humbly beseech you in all these matters and in awe of your greatness beyond my comprehension. Amen.

Meditation Verse: Isaiah 8:1
The Lord said to me, "Take a large scroll and write on it with an ordinary pen."

The One-Page Game Plan

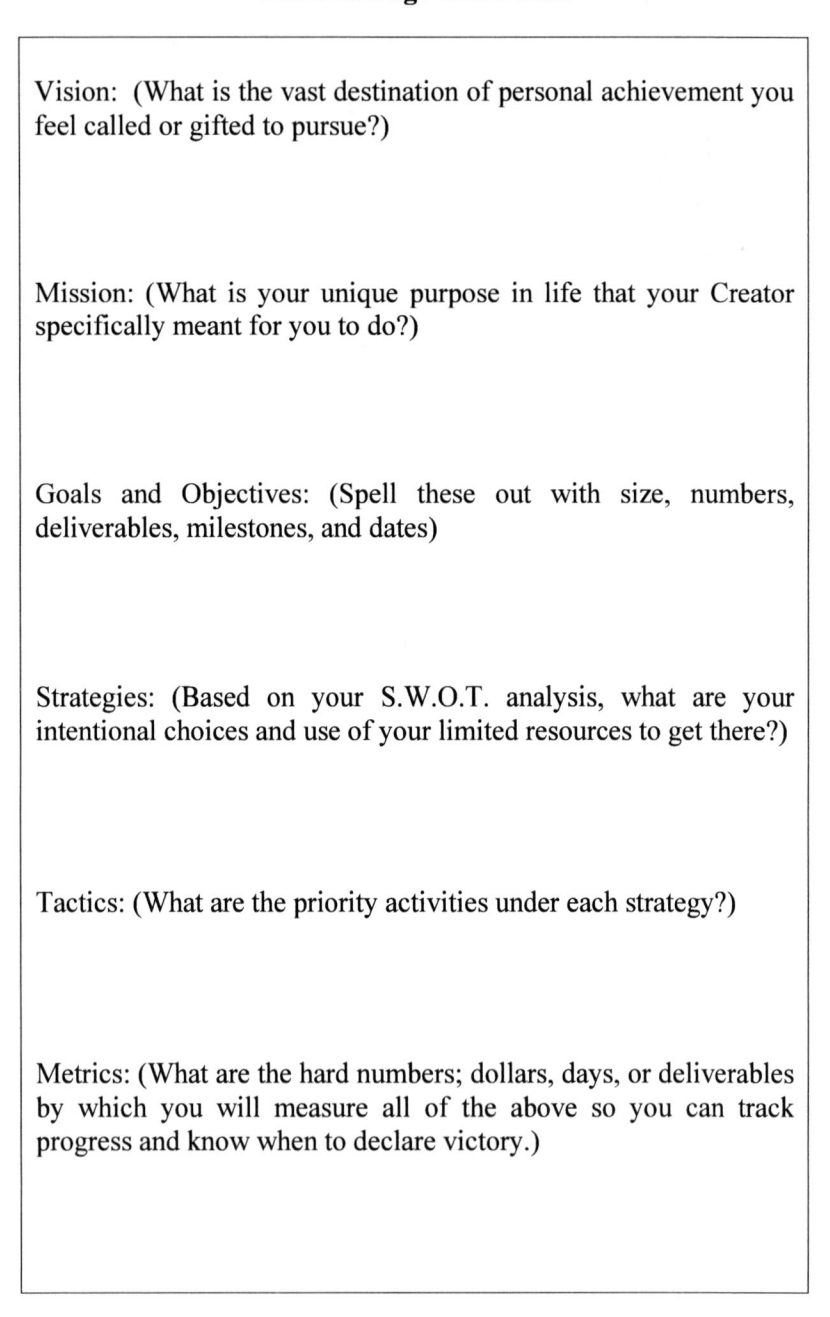

Vision: (What is the vast destination of personal achievement you feel called or gifted to pursue?)

Mission: (What is your unique purpose in life that your Creator specifically meant for you to do?)

Goals and Objectives: (Spell these out with size, numbers, deliverables, milestones, and dates)

Strategies: (Based on your S.W.O.T. analysis, what are your intentional choices and use of your limited resources to get there?)

Tactics: (What are the priority activities under each strategy?)

Metrics: (What are the hard numbers; dollars, days, or deliverables by which you will measure all of the above so you can track progress and know when to declare victory.)

CHAPTER 4

Focus On The Vision

"Focus or it's hopeless."

FOCUS EQUALS ONE THING

Even with a clear game plan in your head and a one-page game plan on paper, life makes it very easy to lose focus. The natural laws of life– inertia, momentum, gravity, complexity– will pull you in many directions or, unconsciously, in the wrong direction.

Fear is a huge foe of focus. Focus equals one commitment, choice, discipline. Fear says "spread the bets; answer all the sideline voices." Fear leads you to feel a need to respond to all the emails, cell phones and other distractions when they often have little to do with vision or mission. Focus equals committing your all and that of your team towards the Vision.

FOCUS AND THE 20/80 RULE

Vilifredo Paretto was an Italian economist of the 19th century who is generally credited with identifying the 20/80 rule which has come to be known as the Paretto Principle. Paretto observed that there was a 20/80 rule in economics but it is also true about most realms of our daily existence. For example:

If you do not believe in the 20/80 rule, or if the Paretto Principle has not yet become part of your unconscious competence, then do a little homework and verify for yourself. [Disclaimer: it may not be exactly 20/80...it may be 25/77 or 15/90...the point is all about observing and knowing disproportionate relationships of activities and events!]

- o U.S. Government statistics! 20% of the people make 80% of the money– at least.
- o Sports pages: 20% of the athletes hit 80% of the home runs or score the most points– at least.
- o If you invest in a 100 new stocks, 20 will generate upwards of 80% of your portfolio growth.

- Less than 20% of the people you know probably give you over 80% of your life joy
- Less than 20% of the people you know probably give you over 80% of your life strife.

What are the Paretto points in your quest towards a Grander Vision? You should continuously be asking yourself where you can focus your time, energy, and resources in pursuit of executing a strategy to hit goals and objectives that get you one step closer to an audacious size vision.

FOCUS ALLOWS MARSHALLING OF RESOURCES
Marshal all resources– time, people, money, personal energy, network.

An army of 3,000 going up against an army of 10,000 does not have a very good chance of prevailing or even surviving. So, what the knowledgeable commander does is look for the weakest points in this larger opponent. Where can his 3,000 knock off 100; 500; or 1,000 of this overwhelming threat? Robert E. Lee was among the best at this approach.

You need to take the same approach with your limited time, talent, team, and resources, versus the overwhelming army of choices, confusion, and competition– no matter what your endeavor.

What part of the day are you most productive? (20/80)

What task gives you the most energy? (20/80)

What teammates are the most productive (20/80)

What problems are the biggest threat? (20/80)

Who are the biggest energy reducers in your life– avoid, neutralize, re-assign, or replace (20/80)

Identify your own Paretto points and marshal your resources here.

FOCUS EQUALS LEVERAGE

Leverage is a state where one input produces a huge multiplier of outputs. Picture the boulder that cannot be budged but with a good strong plank as a lever you can move it because your same body now has a lot of leverage.

There are time, money, and people moments that produce opportunities for leverage.

Identify these moments as part of your Paretto analysis and then marshal your resources against them. You will move personal mountains with these focused planks. We will talk more about leverage shortly. Stay tuned.

FOCUS OR IT'S HOPELESS

I minimize the use of absolute statements, but I truly believe that, in the pursuit of a grander vision, the truth is: "Focus or it is truly hopeless!" It is hopeless to think you will ever overcome all the natural drag and brokenness of life to achieve anything of significance unless you force yourself to focus.

My friend, Bob Hanlon, is 100% passionate and focused on his calling and career as a Financial Planner. He has hundreds of clients and has been at this trade for over 20 years. Most of his clients have found financial success, life significance, or both. At one of our sessions, Bob said to me with absolute conviction from experience, "Bill, I have observed that there is one difference between those with financial security vs. those who have not achieved it, and that one thing is... FOCUS."

FOCUSED VISION
AND THE POWER OF THE ONE-PAGE GAME PLAN

In the previous chapter, we introduced the concept of the one-page game plan. The one-page game plan can be incredibly powerful in helping to harness the vision. A creative or driven mind wants to go in multiple directions at all times. Everything seems important or appears to have some role in the pursuit of the Vision. And, to some extent, it may. But too often, these are non-productive distractions.

An important part of the power of the one-page game plan is that it can crystallize your thought processes. You can develop the habit of using it as a tool that you pick up each day. You either execute against it or modify it or both. But you do not allow your work energy to be dissipated towards distractions. You develop the discipline to drive off of the one page game plan.

IT BECOMES YOUR PERSONAL ROAD MAP AND GAME PLAN

From the early recording of history, military commanders have worked off battle plans. They would carry them around, spread them on a big table, and execute against the plan. Alexander the Great, George Patton, Joan of Arc, Colin Powell– you can picture them doing this.

Professional football coaches pace the sidelines with their game plans honed and refined each week for a new opponent. They have a plan. They don't make it up as they go along.

Architects and builders, masons, carpenters all operate off a blueprint. They do not come to the job site and make it up. They don't say, "I think we will throw some bricks here and let's put a window there." Of course they don't. They operate off a written plan and so should you. Your plan is the one-page game plan.

It allows you, as leader, to personally communicate the vision, the strategy, and plan that leads to victory. Your first challenge is to get yourself straight. You need to know where you are going and what you are pursuing with your life this year, quarter, month, week, and day.

Now, you can do the same for your team and followers. Your personal power comes from chopping up the huge assignment into smaller pieces and delegating out the assignment into readily absorbable pieces. And, the assignments are all consistent with the One-Page Game Plan. Once again, you have taken a complex situation and translated it into simple doable tasks.

IT GIVES YOUR TEAM THE BIG PICTURE

Once you, as the leader, have developed the good habit of living by the one-page game plan, now you have now won the right to lead by example. Encourage your teammates to put the One-Page Game Plan on their wall, in their personal organizers, and under their pillows! A good friend and key mentor, Dr. Stephen Payne, says that visions need to go up on a pedestal and be visible to all. Everybody needs to have it in their face continuously because, unfortunately, it is all too often true that out of sight is out of mind.

I agree and believe one way to do this is by focusing your team's energy and priorities on the one-page game plan. Carry it around. Start progress updates with it. Build respect for it. It will create huge leverage.

PRIORITIZE: BIG THINGS FIRST

It is easy to spend all of your days on little stuff that everybody else wants you to do. Your big challenge is to say "no" to all of these temptations and challenges and to stay focused on the Big; the First Things; the highest contribution points you can make. (See Stephen Covey and *First Things First*).

THE CASCADE OF DREAM, VISION, STRATEGY, TACTICS AND EXECUTION

There is a cascade that looks like the following:

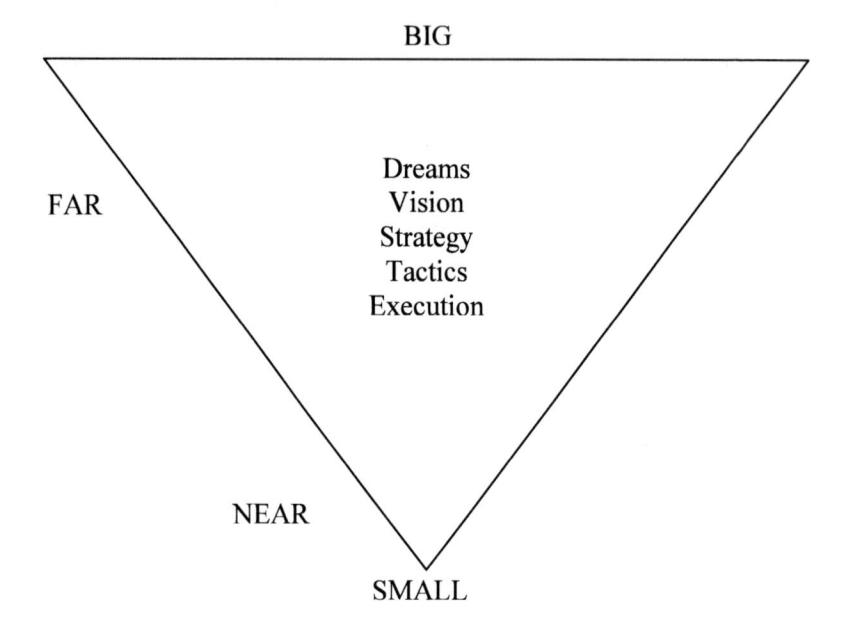

```
              BIG

FAR      Dreams
         Vision
         Strategy
         Tactics
         Execution


     NEAR
              SMALL
```

Dreams are big, far, vague, fuzzy.

Vision is a dream taking shape. You can actually get it on paper.

Strategy is a choice of how to pursue the vision.

Tactics are the programs, projects, activities, and tasks that align with the strategy.

Execution is getting the task done well and on time.

PROJECTS AND ACTIVITIES ARE THE DAILY BUILDING BLOCKS TOWARD THE BIG DREAM.

It can be a lot of fun to dream. But if you do not get to work and move continuously in action mode against the plan, you will awaken one day depressed with nothing to show but an empty dream.

To give some perspective, the dream may be a 10-20 year horizon. The vision is a tangible state 5-10 years out. Strategy can be 1-3 years but may need revision as the overall situation changes. Tactics are within the year, and execution is a function of work ethic, best practices, and attention to detail on a daily basis.

Work ethic means that I do whatever I have to do to get the job done. Maybe it is 6 hours someday when life ensues; other days it is 16 hours. It is what it is– to hold up commitments and deliver quality output on time.

Some of the critical best practices referenced above include: hiring the right people for the right positions; creating strategy from strength; resourcing to win; empowering people to make decisions; creating an atmosphere of positive and energizing accountability.

"Attention to detail" is different than micromanaging. Attention to critical detail is a coveted leadership trait. If there is a hairline fracture in a gas tank of an airplane on an assembly line, well, that is a critical detail. Managing who plays tennis on the White House tennis courts as one of our presidents was alleged to have done fits the category of micromanaging.

PRIORITIZE YOUR ACTIVITIES AND THAT OF YOUR TEAM AROUND THE FIRST, THE BIG AND THE CRITICAL.

- o First things first: There are only 24 hours in a day and, often, with meetings, travel, phone time, and other commitments, you may only have 1-2 hours in a day to get something done. Commit to identify and create a personal discipline to focus on…

- BIG things first: It is easy to get sucked into the urgent trivialities. It is tough and anxiety-producing to ignore them. But you can learn and it will be quite liberating.

- Critical success factors: Start each day with a small index card or back of a business card and write down the four most important things (task, phone call, written report, whatever) that must get done. Do them first or do them in between urgent trivialities, or delay your bone-weary body going to bed. But make a commitment to yourself that you will do them.

FOCUS ON LEVERAGE AND SYNERGY OPPORTUNITIES

Leverage and synergy are related and have some overlap, but are not the same phenomena. But they are critical concepts to understand. People who pursue leverage and synergy accomplish so much more with their time, life, leadership, and results than those who do not. Leverage and synergy are the big exponential multipliers of inputs that result in extremely disproportionate outputs. Let's look at further below.

Leverage

Leverage is a wonderful state where one unit of input produces ten units of output. Money, per se, is a great example. You can put $1,000 in a bank money market and make 1% annual interest, which would produce for you $10 of additional value at the end of the year. Or, you could be the fortunate executive in the right place with the right new product concept who puts the same $1,000 into the stock founding a new company at a penny a share. For that one cent per share, he now owns 100,000 shares. If and when that company goes public at, say, $20/share, the original $1,000 is now worth $2million. This is simple leveraged math. In the first case, there is a $10 output. In the second case, there is a $2million output. That is leverage. Now, admittedly, in the case of the money market, you sleep while you are making the $10 and, in the case of the executive founding the company, you work your tail off 24/7 to make it happen. But anyway you cut it, this is leverage.

Let me take it to a more practical level. Let's say you have an opening in your organization and you have to fill the slot. You are going to spend maybe ten hours of total preparation and interview and follow-up. Coming out of that, you are going to hire someone who will work 2-3,000 hours per year on behalf of you and the organization. If done right and you make a great hire, can you see the leverage here?

It has been my observation over thirty plus years in the business world, that senior executives have found the way to create leverage and synergy and this is a key reason they produce exceptional results. Speaking of...let's talk about synergy.

Synergy

Synergy is that wonderful phenomena where 1+1=3. This simple equation captures the magic where separate factors, forces, or entities come together to create more than there is when they exist apart. Again, my experiential definition of synergy is *where separate factors, forces, or entities come together to create more than there is when they exist apart.* If you are familiar with synergy, this is obvious. If you are not, let me give some examples and then go away and discover all the opportunities for synergy in your life and leadership situation.

- Pharmaceutical company A in North Jersey has an awesome R&D operation, discovering miraculous and innovative new compounds that turn into drugs. But they have no commercialization capabilities, so they have to give away 30% of their profits to a partner who can provide this. Pharmaceutical company B in South Jersey has an awesome juggernaut of sales, marketing, and commercialization but no R&D capability. They have to give away 30% of profits to procure products from other innovators. The two companies decide to merge. They shed redundant operations resulting in three facilities instead of six, one switchboard operator instead of two, etc. Each is no longer giving away 30% of profits to a third party and profits go up 50% in the combined entity. Simply, 1+1=3, or, synergy!

- Church A has a great preacher but terrible music and a congregation of 300. Church B has a terrible preacher but a great music program and a congregation of 200. Pastor B decides to retire and the elders decide to merge with Church A. The new church has such vibrancy that the congregation grows to 1000 members. The synergy equation is 300+200=1000.

- Bob is single and miserable. Mary is single and miserable. They meet each other and fall in love and get married. Over the next 50 years, they procreate 5 children and 15 grandchildren and 30 great grandchildren. After they die, their legacy continues as these offspring generate 90 more great great grandchildren. In my estimation, that is synergy of the highest order. 1+1=140 plus in this example!

Where are the synergy points in your life, your world, your family, your job, your leadership, or your faith? Look for them. They are there and waiting for you to exploit them as opportunities for transformation.

FOCUS EQUALS AN INTENSE CONCENTRATION OF YOUR BEING ON ONE THING

The nature of life and existence is to diffuse, confuse, and overwhelm the senses. Fears and anxieties make us hop from one little task to another, putting our fingers in dikes to hold back imaginary floodwaters. Or, life can look like an illusion of a banquet with so many delectable choices to pursue. We want them all. But life is inherently broken. Things don't work. People don't work. They disappoint too often.

Gravity is a natural law for celestial objects. And, there is a gravity that works against FOCUS in your life. FOCUS is at the top of the world. Gravity wants to pull you down into the netherworld of endless choices, urgent trivialities, must-dos, have to dos, more to-dos, mortgage payments, late bills, and what others want you to do.

Then fear and anxiety kick in. The little voice whispers, "Focus equals commitment." If you commit all to one, you are left exposed on many fronts. Due to fear of failure, you hesitate committing to one thing.

So, you are left with the critical life choices of what to do with your limited resources of 100 hours, 100 dollars, and 100 people. I use 100 to keep it simple. Where and how will you deploy your fixed resources? Will you play the game of life as though on defense? Will you spread your bets, cover all risks, think small, and prepare for endless rainy days? Or, will you go for it and commit your one and only life to something BIG?

What does BIG look like? It has huge value to you personally, and your fellow human beings collectively. You do not need to be setting your sights at the level of Bill Gates or Billy Graham, although that would be terrific. It could be that you feel called to be a nurse, or an elementary school teacher, or a full-time stay at home parent. Each of these are big ideas as long as you see the huge connection to your fellow human beings. And, you go into the pursuit with the intent that you are going to be the best; you will give it your all; you will "leave it on the floor," in the words of a popular Gatorade basketball commercial.

In recent years, I have made it a practice to attend the three-day Leadership Summit held in mid-August at Willow Creek Community Church in Barrington, Illinois. Willow Creek is a BIG IDEA and the inspired brainchild of the founder and senior pastor, Bill Hybels. Bill Hybels founded "Willow" in a movie theatre with a handful of followers about 25 years ago.

Today, Willow Creek Community Church is a sprawling campus and enterprise that serves over 18,000 congregates on weekend services and has set itself up through the Willow Creek Association to be a best practices resource to churches throughout the world. The Leadership Summit is a gathering of Christian lay leaders and pastors who meet to sharpen their leadership skills in building the kingdom of God on earth.

Bill Hybels can be counted on to regularly prick his audience of leaders to think BIG. I remember a recent prodding; "Don't fish for small things, fish for BIG things. Don't fish for perch, fish for people." That is, in essence, what Jesus said to Peter and James when he recruited them and what Bill Hybels paraphrased to the leadership gathering. Drop your perch lines. Join my transformational revolution and I will make you fishers of men.

I confess that I continuously struggle to try and think that big, that selfless. My FOCUS for most of my life has been money, material acquisition, and comfort. OK, throw in protection and survival. Did I mention total self-absorption? You get the picture.

And what is wrong with all of the above? There is nothing inherently wrong. Much of it is actually quite nice. But, in terms of FOCUS and centering on that ONE THING that should have huge value to you personally and your fellow human beings collectively… it just doesn't cut it.

"Do not store up for yourselves treasures that rust or that moths devour. But store up for yourselves treasures in heaven." So said the Master Teacher.

How is this for an epitaph –
>Wore nice clothes.
>Stayed warm.
>Hands stayed pretty clean.
>Nice Car.
>Few weeds in the lawn.
>Saw spouse and kids periodically at the end of a ragged day… while pursuing perch.

I am probably being a little harsh, but not too much. In any event, I am trying to coax you and me out of the comfort zone of… comfort. In high school and college, I worked out with weights regularly. I hated the bench press; on my back, pumping towards the ceiling. Thirty-some years ago, I wrote on the ceiling of my basement in charcoal as a motivational tagline, "No Pain, No Gain." I visited my parents home recently and the words are still there. The words are still true. The opposite of pain is comfort.

"Lose your life and you will gain it. Gain your life and you will lose it."

Focus equals one thing! "No man can serve two masters for he will love the one and hate the other." You must focus on one big thing.

FOLLOW YOUR INSTINCTS

Most people have dreams; big dreams. Unfortunately, too often these ideas are dead on arrival by the time they reach the part of the psyche that borders on action. And dreams without actions are fantasies. Go with your inner instincts for pursuing something big. Don't let fear and anxiety stop you from even constructing a launching pad.

These dreams are a reflection of what we really want to do with our lives, of the life we truly desire to live. But then we kill them as self-talk sets in. "I can never become president of the United States or CEO of a major corporation; a doctor, lawyer, or self-employed entrepreneur; or a famous writer, explorer, teacher. I can never become a nurse, artist, or writer, or professor, or researcher. Just not possible."

Why not?

And then we list all of the obstacles standing in the way. Some are clear, some are vague. We immediately calculate what would be required to achieve any of these goals. "There aren't enough hours in the day. There aren't enough lives to live."

This becomes the first line of defeatist thinking. Maybe, the real conversation going on inside is something like this: "To pursue my dream; my inner calling; my instincts, would mean I would have to focus all my time and energy on this dream or life goal or aspiration. And then what if it doesn't work out? Oh, woe is me, what then am I left with?"

ANSWER:

If it doesn't work out, you will be left with the following:
- A great journey
- Spending your life doing what you really felt called to do
- Meeting new people and finding new skills
- Learning important life lessons

- A tremendous boost in self-confidence, knowing you were one of the few with the courage to pursue a dream
- A launching pad for next dream or your second shot at the stars.

FOLLOW YOUR PASSION

There should be passion and vision, a sense of calling, a connection with your innate gifts, an internal desire that propels your focus. Ultimately, and sooner than later in your maturation process, you want to get to a place where you are connecting with God and getting in touch with God's unique purposes for your creation and what you are to do with your life.

I told you earlier how I had majored in biology/pre-med in college. Then and now, I still have a passion about the biological mysteries of life. I am completely blown away by electron microscopy, biochemical pathways in the body, genetics, DNA, protein synthesis.

For me, it is a connection to God. I see God's hand all over it. Admittedly, many others, when confronted with the same evidence, come to a very different conclusion. But I will leave it to them to explain their positions.

So, I have always had a calling to biology; the study of life. It is clear now that I have the perspective of looking backwards. I love how pharmaceuticals crack the code of optimal safety and efficacy with chemicals found in nature. These potentially dangerous substances are then reconfigured and extensively tested through science to produce little miracles in a bottle that preserve, improve, or save lives. It is all about the sanctity of life. I did not know any of this when I enrolled in biology a long time ago. But it was imbedded in my unique makeup endowed to me by my Creator.

That has carried on and into an absolute core belief about the sanctity of life; the preciousness; the value, the purpose, and the connection of all life to the Creator of life.

But back to the college major for a moment. I was enrolled in biology/pre-med. I definitely had a calling about the biology, but I did not have a calling about the pre-med part. As I previously alluded to, with decades under my belt and looking back into a very clear rear-view mirror, I can identify the three reasons I wanted to become a doctor:

1. People would respect me
2. I would make a lot of money
3. My parents and grandparents would be very proud

There is nothing inherently wrong with the three points above. But they are not about calling or gifting. And, they will not propel or energize you for very long. I had no huge inner drive to become a doctor. Truth be told, I do not like dealing with bodily fluids, messiness, the aging process, sleepless nights, being on-call, or touching diseased people. I am giving you a true confession.

And, I have enormous respect and gratitude for doctors, nurses, and other healthcare practitioners who have been called into a continuation of the work of Jesus Christ; the master healer and doctor of all times.

But doctor is not me. Biology is me. There is a connection, a calling, a purpose, and a vision. Important lesson: There is a major distinction between a calling (biology, the study of life) and a profession, such as a doctor. And, once you get this straight; once you are clear on your calling, passion and unique gifts, then you are at a fantastic place to bring leverage, synergy, and focus on a powerful vision. Now, all of your investment of time and energy will not just be work, it will be fueled by and to the ends of a significant purpose.

Questions For Reflection:

1. What would you pursue if you were 100% certain that you could not fail? What is holding you back?

2. In the words of Lloyd Ogilvie, author of *Lord of the Impossible*, "what would you attempt if you were sure that the Lord would intervene to help you?" If you knew that you absolutely could not fail at a pursuit because the Creator of the Universe was backing you, what would that pursuit or endeavor be?

3. What is stopping you from fully putting your focus on this pursuit?

4. What is the one thing you would love to do (or accomplish) that you haven't done?

5. What is the Grander Vision of your life? Can you commit to making this happen?

6. Create your one-page game plan for your grander vision of your life.

Prayer

Dear Lord, I beseech you to find favor in your servant and provide me with the gifts of faith and focus. Allow me to focus all of my energies on what is important to you and give me the faith to pursue it fearlessly.

Meditation Verse: Proverbs 3:5-6
"Trust in the Lord with all your heart and lean not on your own understanding."

CHAPTER 5

Energize Your Team

As Jesus was walking beside the Sea of Galilee, he saw two brothers, Simon, called Peter, and his brother, Andrew. They were casting a net into the lake, for they were fishermen. "Come follow me," Jesus said, "and I will make you fishers of men." At once, they left their nets and followed him.
- Matthew 4:18-20

MOTIVATING PEOPLE

Reflect on the following statement: "Teams are comprised of people." Say that again until it sinks in. Now you will not be frustrated or disappointed as you encounter one innate obstacle after another in attempting to motivate a team– of people.

They are fellow human beings who, just like you and me, suffer from greed, insecurity, frustrations, competitiveness, comparisons, and, dare do I say, covetousness. They want to know what you can do for them. Into this challenge doth plunge you, the daring leader, with a grander vision. But it can be done and we will explore the ways and means below in this chapter.

RECRUITING

Senior executives and other super-achievers spend their time with a keen focus and prioritization on the most important goal, or endpoint, they are pursuing. They prioritize or select the use of their time on tasks that have the greatest potential for leverage or synergy.

In ancient times, Archimedes said, "Give me a lever and I will move the world." This phrase has often been depicted with a normal-looking individual moving a huge boulder with a plank of wood leveraged beneath it. In virtually any business or organization, the critical activities of recruiting, identifying, courting, and hiring the key individuals of your team are likely the most leveraged use of your time. You will move mountains when you do it right or get buried in an avalanche when you mess up in this most important area.

RETAINING

I believe that 80% of retention is based on proper recruiting. Recruit with the following four key factors in mind:

1. INTEGRITY- Does the candidate have 100% integrity and honesty? If yes, proceed further; if not, terminate and do not waste another moment of your highly-valuable time. And, whatever you do, avoid rationalizing that perhaps the person will change and learn honesty in the future, etc.

2. COMPETENCY- Can they achieve the results expected of the job based on their prior work/life track record and relevant references? Can you project them growing into much larger responsibilities down the line? What is their energy and ambition level?

3. CHEMISTRY- Is there chemistry between you and the recruit? Are you going to want to spend a lot of time with this person and share soul-searing trials along the journey?

4. CULTURE- Is there a cultural fit with the other team members and the overall organization? Every organization has a culture, that is, a set of beliefs and behaviors, customs and practices. For example, if the culture is neat, punctual, and formal, there will be a disconnect with a recruit who is sloppy, late, and informal.

This is not to say that you recruit a bunch of clones for your team. To the contrary, you want a broad range of diverse experience, management, and leadership styles on your team. This provides depth and strength. But the recruit either has to fit into the current culture or display the traits of the new culture you, as the leader, are attempting to create anew in the organization.

If you focus on these four things up front in recruiting, you have a significantly increased probability of retaining your valued team members down the line when strife, disappointment, and setbacks inevitably occur.

Help and teach them to follow the same principles as they begin to hire.

CONSTRUCTING TEAMS

Let me share some thoughts on constructing teams from two perspectives which are first, when you have inherited a team, and second, when you are staffing from scratch. In both cases, there are core principles, such as:

- How do I get more speed, decision-making, innovation, creativity, productivity, and esprit de corps out of this group as a result of them coming together than if they worked apart?

- How is the chemistry of the group? Arguing and debating, shouting and passion are good. But working to undermine one another for personal gain or furthering one's own agenda is destructive.

- Do I have the right people on the team? In asking this, let's think of the concept of team in two magnitudes– your staff of direct reports and any assigned matrix members; this is the BIG team. Then, we are also thinking in terms of all the multitude of ad hoc teams. These are the smaller teams. In both cases, the dynamics of teams are at play.

Next, let's talk about how teams generally get the work done. The obvious answers are team leaders, meetings, and written documents. This is where you, as the leader, can bring leverage and added value, thereby greatly improving the productivity of the group and your own personal productivity.

For the BIG team, YOU are the leader so I am going to shift attention to the smaller teams. But I am assuming that you, as leader of the BIG team, are going to be modeling these best practices.

Team leader

The team leader has to be someone you trust, shares your vision and is working in concert with you. This person does not need to agree with you all of the time or agree with your view of strategy or tactics- while these subjects are up for discussion. In fact, you want someone strong enough to challenge your thinking. It is a Yin/Yang type of thing. They support you but they feel confident enough to challenge you. And you have created a safe and encouraging environment that this is the normative behavior you expect.

The team leader has to be clear on the purpose, crisp deliverable and timeline of the group. I try to ingrain a mantra of "deadlines and deliverables" into the team leaders and all members of the teams.

Meet with the team leader regularly for an update on progress towards the deadlines and deliverables, but you do not have to sit through all the meetings. Do your homework up front in picking the team leaders and the other key members of their teams. Crystallize the purpose of the team and give clear deadlines and deliverables.

Meetings

I know you are groaning at the mention of meetings. Why is that so? Because, like me, you probably think you have wasted about ten good years of your entire life in meetings. I cannot stand group meetings any longer than they have to go on. I start twitching and my right leg starts thumping the ground– if it is a non-productive meeting. But I take this enormous experience of bad meetings into my thinking of how to run highly-effective meetings. It is really about following core principles of highly effective meetings:

1. Have a leader. Somebody has to run the meeting. No group gropes, please.

2. Have an agenda with responsibilities and even the deliverables of the day spelled out in advance. People need to know they are not just showing up for free donuts and coffee, but something productive is expected of them in this time slot, i.e. work!

3. Start on time. You get there on time and start. Let late comers know you would appreciate them being on time. I read constantly how President George W. Bush follows this practice. If he can do this with the scope and responsibility of running the free world, the rest of us can surely do it as well. It is OK to finish ahead of time! For goodness sakes, do not feel compelled to fill the whole allotted time slot. Achieve the purpose of the day and let people go back to have individual productivity time, of which a lot is phone calls and telecommunications with the outside world where the real action is.

4. Start with actions from last meeting that has "deadlines and deliverables" and hold people accountable for commitments they made.

5. End with deadlines and deliverables moving forward to the next meeting. In doing this, you are ingraining a culture of- action, productivity and problem-solving. In the process, you are teaching accountability and an appreciation of how precious time is.

Written Documentation

There is an expression that "an army moves on its belly" which means they not only crawl as in the infantry but that you must feed them too. And your war-fighting will only be as effective as your ability to manage logistics and get the food there.

Workplaces move forward on written documentation. Words disappear, memories are fleeting, and other work pressures intervene. So, having effective written documentation is critical to the effectiveness of teams. I am not a big proponent of "minutes" (unless there is a legal mandate as in boards, etc.) or detailed recitations of who said what. No, the written documentation you want coming out of a meeting should be short telegraphic bullets of– who will do what by when, leading up to the next meeting. Share other background documents as information but do not look for polished reports coming out of all the ad hoc meetings that you, as leader, are sponsoring. You want short crisp action-oriented summaries of burning issues and who will do what by when. Meeting adjourned.

When it comes to the end of a project, nobody is going to read even a twenty-page report. So, make sure you have a well-crafted executive summary of 1-3 pages and a PowerPoint summary in headlines, highlights, and easy-to-grasp bullets. This write-up should be self-explanatory to those who pick it up when the author is not there to explain and fill in the lines and details.

There is an exception to this rule. For highly sensitive, politicized, or extremely difficult situations, or where there may be an otherwise hostile audience, you will do better with a minimum of information on the PowerPoint slides. It is you verbalizing in front of the group that is really the whole story. The less you put up, the better. The more you put up, the more ammunition opponents have to use against you. In this case, just use the PowerPoint bullets as broad headlines. It is a roadmap for you to carry the whole story. You are the leader and, therefore, you are the story. The details are secondary. You should have multiple levels of details as backup information but you are going to attempt to get in and out of a tight situation with a minimum of information.

But in closing on the subject of constructing teams, remember:
- choose an effective team leader first and foremost
- set clear definitions around finished deliverables
- teach them how to run effective meetings
- keep the written report crisp, clear, and action-oriented

FILL THE LEADERSHIP SPACE WITH ENERGY

Hiring well is the first step in recruiting and retaining. But after the person comes on board and the "honeymoon" is long over, your leadership style and substance is the next major factor impacting the outcome.

As leader, a primary role you play is to ***energize the space between you and the people on your team.*** You can do the following things to energize your team:

- Exhibit a positive can-do attitude and expect the same from them

- Be open and accessible

- Listen and suggest solutions

- Be on the ready for teaching and coaching moments

- Continuously give feedback and help people grow

- Constantly clarify the vision and current priorities

- Knock down obstacles for them that only you can knock down

- Get them the resources they need to be successful

- Listen (Did I mention listen?)

- Serve: They are on the team to serve you and produce deliverables but you are also part of the team and need to serve their needs in helping them be successful.

ENERGIZE!

As I write these very passages for the first time, it is a Monday morning. I have cycled through hundreds of people and settled into my wonderful free upgraded first class seat on Continental Airlines at Newark Airport. Did I mention first class? I tell you this not to impress you, but to impress upon you that I am in the midst of the alleged movers and shakers of our country– and they look very exhausted and weary. Hopefully, when we arrive in Los Angeles five hours from now, all will respond to their calling and mandate as leaders to <u>energize</u> the space around them.

I want to emphasize that one of the most unique contributions of the leader is to energize the space around them. That means to energize the space between you and your boss; the space between you and your peers, subordinates, and external agents. It means to energize the space with your customer, community leaders, or suppliers.

All of these people and stakeholders are vital to your success and towards achievement of the grander vision. They work for you whether they realize it or not. They can come at the task as either humdrum or really energized about it. It is your job to fill this leadership space with energy.

"AHAH" INSIGHTS
Show enthusiasm, passion, and commitment for the vision, mission, and purpose at hand. Show a genuine interest for your boss, peer, or team-member in both their work and personal life.

Exhibit a positive can-do attitude no matter how challenging the situation. In crisis, stay balanced, realistic, not rose-tinted, but also positive, can-do, believing, and problem solving. Teach, train, coach, counsel, direct, redirect. Prioritize, communicate, dialogue, show compassion. Use tough love when needed. When you see their eyes and face light up, you have had an "AHAH" moment. Celebrate and congratulate yourself.

When you share a slice of your life or work wisdom and truly communicate a new way of looking at things, this is an "AHAH" insight.

CONSTRUCTIVE FEEDBACK
Imagine for a moment that you were at milepost 10 of a 100-mile road that ended suddenly at a deadly precipice. Imagine also that your boss or teammate knew this but didn't tell you because it might (a) hurt your feelings, or (b) make them uncomfortable – at the thought of hurting your feelings. So, they let you waste 90 more miles and then either let you plunge to your death, or, at the last minute scream, "wait, stop, please... I should have told you 100 miles ago but there is a disaster 100 yards ahead."

With this image in mind, do everybody a favor and give continuous constructive feedback to all on a timely basis. Do not let people waste their time, talent, and resources or yours going in the wrong direction because you might hurt their feelings (or your feelings). Constructively tell them what they need to know to be more successful. They will truly appreciate you for it.

FACILITATIVE LEADERSHIP

Leading by example is critical but it does not mean doing everything yourself. Far from it. As leader, you can be most effective by focusing your energies on BIG issues, like vision, mission, strategy, staffing, and hiring. You need to be organizing the work, setting standards and expectations, and solving the unsolvable daily problems that only you can solve.

Resourcing is another major area of facilitative leadership. Getting, apportioning, managing, and tracking resources is the first and best use of your time in facilitative leadership. Your second best use is to knock down obstacles, redirect the focus, and re-clarify expectations while your teammate is still at milepost 10! Do not wait until they get to the end of the long, wrong road and they are about to fall into the abyss. This is facilitative leadership.

HANDS-ON HELP

And then sometimes there is no better use of your time and energy than direct hands-on help. Some examples of where this is the case are the following:

(1) It now becomes clear, with critical timelines approaching, that you miscalculated the time and resources required of the delegated act and, at this point, only you can do it or your hands-on contribution is a do or die matter.

(2) Somebody else could do it but here is great symbolism, or a motivational moment, by you doing it.

(3) All are working to their fullest and a critical event is approaching, wherein more hands are required. Again, it is critical (not routine). Jump in. Pitch in. Get your hands dirty. Get it done!

CONNECT THE TEAM TO A HIGHER CAUSE

THAN SELF

Years back, I had the privilege of hearing a dinner speech by Charles Garfield, author of *Peak Performers*. One of the vignettes he related stuck in my memory and shaped the way I look at leadership, vision, and motivation. Garfield told the story about a maintenance man at NASA and an exchange that the maintenance man had with a visitor. The dialogue went something like this:

"How long have you been wiping floors here at NASA?" he was asked.

"I don't wipe floors," he replied, "I am helping our country to put a man on the moon."

That is connecting to a higher cause. It is not about connecting to the floor but to the ceiling, the skies, and the moon; literally.

If you really want to connect to a higher cause, then read an NIV (New International Version) Study Bible from cover to cover. The NIV was one of the great undertakings of the 20th century in my humble opinion. It produced a version of the Bible that is totally readable, engaging as though it were an action novel and got sign-off from a multi-denominational panel of experts that the scriptural truths had been maintained. It is also about 40% notes and references of where the content came from which is incredibly fascinating and reinforcing of belief.

If you will take a month or two to read an NIV Bible from cover to cover, it will be the best investment of time you ever made. Among the many benefits, you will see your life and work connected to a higher cause. This is hugely energizing.

RECOGNITION AND REWARDS AS ENERGIZERS

It does not matter if it is a non-profit or for-profit organization; individuals want to receive recognition and rewards for a job well done. You will always have certain constraints on the financial rewards, i.e. 4.0% target pay increases or a fixed target for bonus- 10%, 30%, 100%, depending upon the organization and industry. So within these confines, make sure you are moving the money around from top performers to bottom performers. While your overall targets might be 4.0% on pay raises and a certain percentage for bonus, make sure you have a good dispersion from top to bottom, i.e. the top might get a 10% raise and the bottom gets zero. This approach motivates everyone– the top, the middle, and the bottom. The top feel they got their due. The middle aspires to reach the top. And the bottom performers get moving up or out.

While there are certain constraints on the rewards side, there are virtually no constraints on the recognition side. You can and should look for opportunities to give public accolades to those who do a super job. The larger the audience in which you recognize them, the better– but you can also sprinkle the acclaim in small, informal settings as well. Write personal notes or cards; handwritten is better than electronic and mailing to the home has more impact than leaving it in the person's inbox.

Other ways to recognize and reward include things like: buy them small tokens of appreciation, take them out to lunch, play golf, or give them a plum assignment like representing your company at an industry event.

MICROMOTIVATION

Also, learn what micro motivates them. This is a term derived from the concept of micromarketing, which was a term that meant, "let's not market to all customers as if they are the same, let's tailor our approach and micro market." From this came the lateral thought of, "let's micro motivate our team members." What motivates one may not motivate the other. For one individual, it might be playing golf with you. For another, it is being able to leave 4:00PM on Thursdays to get to a child's soccer game. For another, it might be daycare flexibility. Learn what is the hot button for your team members and seek to tap into micro motivation. It is a high octane reward and recognition approach.

UNDERSTAND THE REALITIES OF POLITICS

In this chapter, we are talking about energizing teams. One of the biggest drains of energy to a team is "politics". Unfortunately, this word is greatly misunderstood and is used more than warranted and often used incorrectly. As a leader, you understand that politics is as ubiquitous as the air we breath. But others do not understand, depending upon their maturity or life experience or personal philosophy of life. So, one of the greatest energizing acts you can give your team is to instruct them on the facts versus the fictions of organizational politics.

Politics has been around since the Garden of Eden. Politics is about who really has the power, who thinks they have the power, and who gets things done through the application of power. It is also about who gets chewed up, spit out, and loses because they are clueless about politics.

I have a friend whose entire career has been as a lawyer in the world of politics. He told me the four things he has learned over the years that shape his thinking about politics are:

1) Politics is the art of taking credit.
2) Politics is the art of dodging blame.
3) All politics is local (people generally only care about themselves and not BIG issues)
4) Politics is all about jobs (whether we are talking who gets the job of President of the United States or who gets one of the last two positions available for township sanitation collector). It is all about jobs.

Politics is a power game, blame game, zero sum, win-lose game as old as creation of humanity itself. In Genesis, God says to Adam, "Who told you it was ok to eat of the tree?" Adam blames the woman and God– "This woman that YOU gave me…" The woman blames the snake– "The snake told me it was OK…" The snake tries to slither off, but not before the wrath and permanent judgment of the Almighty One is rendered. And so, it is played out to this day. Politics is a reality wherever two or more people interact towards a win/lose objective. Politics are not pretty because the behaviors of individuals when they have to operate in the give-and-take of an organization or society are often not pretty. In any organization, you must understand the realities of the politics of your situation.

FACE INTO THE POLITICS OF YOUR SITUATION

I have seen politics in my home growing up, in high school, college, the military, my church, the golf club, and every job or pursuit I have ever had. You probably have, too. So let's all admit up front that politics exist. You cannot pass GO, collect $200, or achieve anything without realizing (vs. denying) that politics exist.

Who has control over your life, money, job, happiness, your performance rating, and your present or future happiness? Think it through. List them. Now understand how you relate to all of them. This is the beginning of understanding and facing into the reality of the politics of your situation.

LEARN HOW TO AT LEAST PLAY DEFENSE IN POLITICS

What is your relationship to each? Are they supportive, friendly, neutral, dangerous, hostile? Enlist the help of those supportive and friendly to your cause. Do well by them. Build up a credit reserve with them.

Some people are obviously dangerous to you. Move these people in the dangerous category to neutral. When I was active in politics, one of the lasting lessons that my mentor taught me was that you want to minimize the size of the group of the people hostile to you and who actively work towards your demise. You want to neutralize these people. Give them something. Usually, it could be something that doesn't cost you money or compromise of your position. It could be as little as just show respect, lend an ear, or give a fair hearing of their point-of-view. Your goal is to move them from dangerous to neutral.

Tread gently around those who are clearly hostile towards you until you have a "stronger hand." Look for allies; there is power in numbers. Consider the wildebeests when the Lion is stalking (political predator). They amass together to minimize sticking out as a target.

Do not antagonize those who are hostile towards you as much as you would probably be tempted to do. If you are certain of the righteousness of your position, then you must hold your ground and ultimately pay a price if necessary. But there is nothing wrong with delaying a painful day of reckoning if you can survive by finding alternative solutions.

GOING ON THE OFFENSE WITH POLITICS (WARNING: DANGEROUS ACTIVITY!)

"Do not fight the king unless you will kill the king." This advice goes back to medieval times and is still true today when it comes to politics. Do not take on your boss, large corporation, chair of the finance committee, or federal government unless one of two things:

    (1) You have a very good chance of prevailing
    (2) You are ready to die

I do not necessarily mean physically die. There are many metaphors in life akin to death. These usually involve painful and or sizable personal loss. There are many subtexts of "death" in the workplace. So, truly know the score and be prepared to handle the downside should you lose your challenge to the political force in your world. It is usually wise to avoid going on the offense in politics unless you have the upper hand and power position or a very good chance of prevailing. Beware!

"A king's wrath is like the roar of a lion. He who angers him forfeits life." (Proverbs 20:2).

One last lesson is important for closing out this session. As people of faith, we are called to "be in this world but not of this world." I have covered the worldly principles of politics above. The lesson from Jesus could be summed up as – do the right thing at all times and let the political chips fall where they may. If you are aligned with God, he will protect you and deliver you to the next step of your journey. Be aware of worldly political forces. Don't spend an overly amount of time on them. Always focus on doing the right thing and leave the outcome in God's hands.

SANITIZE

Periodically, you must clean or sanitize your house, as boring or distasteful as it may seem. So it is in pursuit of your Grander Vision. You must sanitize your head of any cobwebs, fuzzy thinking, or just plain erroneous beliefs. There may be things once true but now false, or false but now true.

Sanitize your eating, drinking, working, playing, and praying habits. Remember the concept of lead by example? So it is with sanitizing. You must sanitize yourself first and continuously, and then you have earned the moral capital and high ground to sanitize your team.

One of my former mentors always tormented me with the lines, "I wouldn't ask you to do anything I wouldn't do myself." Or, "I wouldn't ask you to do what I haven't already done myself." In other words, he was telling me, "I am leading you by my example and so now I expect you to do what I asked of you."

ONE IS EITHER PART OF THE SOLUTION OR PART OF THE PROBLEM

You handpicked your team with the greatest of intentions. But honeymoons in marriage and in work can be short affairs. Over time, reality settles into its own pace and place.

If someone on your team is not getting the job done, or resists coaching and training, or is just in the wrong job or – heaven forbid – is working against you, then you have one choice. It is an easy and clear choice – sanitize. Move the person out to another position, another line of endeavor, or another state. You must! The downside is enormous.

LEADER: SANITIZE YOURSELF FIRST

Is a core belief obsolete? Is your walk not matching your talk? Is your ethical edge fraying? Is your work ethic or focus less than robust? Are you abusing people or your perks or your position of power? You get the idea. Now think of ten similar questions very specific to your situation.

If the answer to any of these questions is yes, take remedial action immediately. It is critical. There is an old Greek expression which summarizes the situation precisely: "The fish rots from the head down."

BE BRUTALLY HONEST WITH YOURSELF ABOUT YOUR TEAM AND SANITIZE AS NEEDED

It is a painful act to move against someone who once was a valued member of your team or you fantasized that they would be someday. It is common to re-fantasize (they will turn around), rationalize (it's not that bad), or even deny (it... it... it can't be). But this is a severe mistake. There is now a cancer growing in the body of your Grand Vision. You must take focused action, or doom is on the horizon.

EFFECTIVELY LEADING "UPWARDS" IS ALSO CRITICAL

So far, we have been focused on leading and energizing subordinates. But in the spirit of 360 degree leadership, you need to put a lot of time and energy into leading up with your boss or bosses. Whereas the four points of the leadership quadrant are up (boss), down (subordinates), sideways (peers and external stakeholders), it is strongly suggested that you put about 50%, not 25%, of your time and energy in leading up. The term "up" can mean an individual boss or it could be an organizational board, or it could be your own personal board of directors. You should recruit and appoint your own personal board of directors just like big corporations do.

CONCEPT OF YOUR PERSONAL BOARD OF DIRECTORS

Why do companies have boards of directors? One reason is that it is law! But there are very practical reasons, too. An effective board should consist of very wise, experienced, and diversely talented people who can help the CEO drive towards the Vision. The best boards supplement areas where the CEO is weak or inexperienced.

I attended several Johnson and Johnson annual stockholder meetings where our CEO would always make it a point to introduce the board and give a face to the stockholders. Members of the board consisted of successful executives, scientists, and individuals who were experts in automobiles, airlines, trains, food, cancer, medicine, politics, and other expertise critical for success on a global scale.

Why shouldn't you have your own personal board of directors who are wise, experienced, and diversely talented and can help you drive towards your personal goals? This is another great place to spend your energy.

HARVEY MCKAY ON DRILLING FOR WATER

Dig Your Well Before You're Thirsty is the title of an informative and entertaining book by Harvey Mackay. It is an excellent "how-to" on developing a broad network of influential people.

The main point of his book is that you must not wait until that critical point where you need a job, a reference, or an infusion of capital to start thinking about your network. It takes a lot of time, caring, and sharing. Start now (drilling). Do not wait until you absolutely have your back up against the proverbial wall (thirsty).

Look around your world of who you know who knows someone else; someone you would like on your personal board of directors. Review your personal and work vision and mission. Who has already blazed the trail where you want to go? Seek these people out.

HOW TO CULTIVATE YOUR NETWORK

Cultivate the habits of confidence, clarity, and conciseness and you will have a high level of success in recruiting, developing, and expanding your network.

Confidence – exhibit the inward and outward projection that you are passionate, committed, and invested in your cause.

Clarity – show them your one-page game plan. They will be very impressed.

Conciseness – the successful people you want as part of your network place a premium on time. After the obligatory informal talk and social banter, get to the point and specifically communicate on where you need their help and advice. Tell them in no uncertain terms what it is you are asking for. This is no time to be shy or coy.

THE POWER OF YOUR NETWORK

Initially go for a 30-minute meeting if you are having difficulty getting on the schedule of a very influential contact. The meeting will likely go 45-60 minutes if you are engaging once you get in. I can think of numerous occasions where the VIP said to the effect that their schedule was packed and if you want to see me, come in at 6:30AM. I have had surgeons ask me to meet them 5:30AM before their patient care starts. My response, "No problem; whatever it takes."

Working lunches are a necessary way to cultivate your network because so many of the types of people you are seeking do not "do lunch," or for them it is a working lunch. Personally, for two reasons, I prefer early morning breakfast meetings when someone wants to meet with me. One, I am open, creative, and fresh in the morning. Two, once my day gets started and I have a head of steam or momentum going, I do not like to stop for lunch and working lunches are my habit.

Even though you are often seeking out people who have more experience or achievement than yourself, you can still give them something of value in return. They are often looking for new leads for their own ventures and you will be surprised with each passing year how your ability here increases.

By focusing on developing a broad network and your own personal board of directors, you will be amazed at the very interesting people you meet. You will grow and move towards your goals in so many ways. If they do not directly help you, usually they refer you to someone else who has vital information, contacts, or know-how. It is an exciting and fun part of leadership. You will be amazed at the talented and gifted individuals you will meet.

As you get to know them, at least two things will happen. One, you will raise the bar on your own expectations about life, business, success, and significance. I have come away from many a network meeting feeling like a massive underachiever. But it stimulated me to raise the bar! The second thing that will happen is that you will get a confidence boost as you relate where you are to where these people have come from. You will be simultaneously impressed with their accomplishments but gain in confidence that you can do it, too.

THE NEED FOR CONTINUOUS UPGRADING OF YOUR NETWORK

I am not advocating using people and tossing them aside. What I am stating is that, with the passing of time and the incremental achievement of goals, you need even wiser, more experienced, more talented, and most importantly, more focused people in your orbit.

Of significant value, your current board can open doors to who is on their board and on and on.

Finally, in terms of downside management, that is, should you find yourself fired, out of money or vision-obliterated, you want a board who can open the next new door – fast.

Questions For Reflection:
1. Am I an energetic leader? Do I have an abundance of energy? Do I spread that energy around to my team in a positive fashion?

2. In terms of personal disciplines (see chapter 2), do I need to change any of my practices to increase my energy?

3. Am I taking the time to face into interpersonal conflicts on my teams and providing constructive feedback?

4. Besides leading "downwards," am I spending enough time practicing 360 degree leadership upwards with my boss or bosses or boards?

5. How am I doing with my personal Board of Directors? Am I cultivating experts, mentors and advisors?

Prayer
Lord, I pray for energy. Help me live a disciplined life that increases my energy level. And then I pray for inspiration and discernment that I would use that energy most constructively with my team, my boss and my personal board of directors.

Meditation Verse: Proverbs 15:22
"Plans fail for lack of counsel but with many advisors they succeed."

CHAPTER 6

Marshal Scarce Resources

"Tempest Fugit. Carpe Diem!"

MANAGING TIME: THE UNIVERSAL 168

The ancient Latin expression above translates to, "Time flies. Seize the day!" In discussing the concepts of scarce resources, I believe that the scarcest and most precious resource of the leader is: time. There are and always will be exactly 168 hours in a week which is universally given to all. So, the question I chronically obsess over is: How do some individuals achieve so much and others so little with the same amount of time?

Here is my best answer:

Those who get the most out of a single week–

- Practice focus
- Know when they are at their personal best and worst and manage it around the 24-hour clock
- Are disciplined to stick to a plan driven by goals and objectives
- Maximize the principles of leverage and synergy
- Understand the power of delegating and managing versus doing themselves
- Practice the concept of energy bursts
- Understand first things first
- Are driven by either an inner demon or a higher cause

WHY DO SOME DO SO MUCH WITH THE SAME 168 HOURS?

It is about discipline and having a plan that predetermines what you want to get out of the day and the week. You have your agenda. Before the emails, phone calls, drop-ins, crises, and family emergencies intervene to throw you off course, you know your agenda for the day. You have willpower and the flexibility to adjust to achieve. But you have YOUR plan and agenda. If you have to get up at 4:00 a.m., skip lunch or push back bedtime, you are resolute to achieve your agenda as the world and its negative forces of gravity, confusion, intrusion, and commotion tries to sink your best laid plans.

IT IS ABOUT CHOICES

Your control over time all starts with the attitude you bring to the subject. You have two choices:

1. Be on offense. You can choose an attitude of gratitude, willpower, intentionality, and a focus on results. You are controlling the ball and the game, to use a football analogy.

OR

2. Be on defense. You can choose an attitude of whatever. Whatever happens was bound to happen, is out of my control, "I am a victim of circumstances." Unfortunately, this usually means that you are on defense, in responsive mode and backpedaling all day.

The people intent on achieving a grand vision for their lives choose the first approach.

FIRST THINGS FIRST AND THE SCHWAB 4

Stephen Covey has authored two excellent best sellers which I recommend all grander vision seekers to read. These two books are, *The 7 Habits of Highly Effective People* and *First Things First*. In the latter book, he makes the point loud and clear that you need to make choices of what is most important to achieve any goals you set and that as the title states, it is incumbent upon you to do "first things first".

Another must-read that reiterated this point is *Think and Grow Rich* by Napoleon Hill. In this book, Hill relates the story about Charles M. Schwab, who, in the 1930s, was the head of Bethlehem Steel. When asked "what was the best management tip he ever learned," Mr. Schwab shared the following: start each day with a card that lists only the four to six most important things that must happen TODAY. (I have chosen four because as you know by now, I am a big fan of FOCUS!) And I have also adopted the filter of "what are the four most important tasks that contribute towards a transformational vision of the future. In other words, what for today are building blocks of something truly significant, or of a grander vision! Decide on them and commit that you will do them. If somebody or something throws another task at you this day, do not do it unless it is more important than what you have on the list. Do not go to bed until you have completed them. In my own mind, I have come to refer to this list as the "Schwab 4." It is an important habit that has become a regular practice for me. I purchased what looks like a lifetime supply of pocket-sized index cards. On one, I list all the phone calls I need to make for the week. Another has the top ten vision-focused tasks that have to get done soon. And the third card has the top four "first things first" list of the day. Do I achieve it 100% of the time? No. Do I go to bed weary and not fully successful some days? Sure. But I achieve my first things first list more often than not and it has become an ingrained habit at this point in my life.

THE CONCEPT OF ENERGY BURSTS

I have mentioned Bill Hybels and Willow Creek several times at this point. And I have been to Willow Creek several times. The size, scope, and feel of the place are breath-taking and inspiring. It is also a crushing management and leadership challenge. While Bill Hybels title is Senior Pastor, I view him more like the CEO of this sprawling global and eternal venture. Certainly, Bill must be swamped in paperwork and minutiae with little time for anything else you would think.

And yet, as I have listened to Bill talk about his life, these snippets come into view. Bill is an avid runner and finds time to run most every day. He makes time for Bible and prayer and journaling most every day. He has a major passion about sailing and owns a refurbished family sailboat which he pursues as often as weather permits. As I mused on all of this, I wondered, how do some do so much with their time and others so little? I wondered, how does Bill do it? I garnered an insight into these questions at one of the annual Willow Creek Leadership Summits hosted each year where Bill introduced for me anyway the concept of energy bursts.

What is an energy burst? It is the following approach to planning your week and your day. You ask yourself questions like:

"When am I at my best?"

"What projects have the most explosive leverage to move the vision forward?"

"What critical tasks must happen because they are mission-critical, big ideas, or have synergy effecting large parts of the venture?"

These are energy bursts. Schedule them first. Commit to them. Prayer and Bible and working out are energy bursts. Schedule them first. Other examples of energy bursts might be some of the following examples.

Suppose you have to write an important speech or make an important presentation. Put it on the calendar and block it out as a formal meeting with yourself and schedule it where you are at your best. I do 90% of my writing between 4:30am and 7:30am. I am juiced up, have a clear head, and most of the world has not gotten revved up. It is my writing energy burst.

Another form of energy bursts that I utilize are breakfast meetings outside the office with people important to my personal or organizational vision. These may be experts, mentors, role-models, consultants, members of my personal board of directors, or multiple roles within these descriptions. And, I usually have a burning question I am trying to get answered which they are uniquely qualified to provide. Or, they know others who have the answer.

So, I try to plan my week with the following energy bursts:

4:30am-6:30am: This is prime time to write, pray, get into the Bible, or work out. It varies by day.

6:30am-7:00am: breakfast with my son before he leaves early for school

I am then usually in the office by 7:30am. I do not eat lunch most days unless they are group lunches. I use 12:00-1:00pm as an energy burst opportunity to work out if I missed it in the morning.

I will bring a sandwich and Diet Coke to a 1:00pm meeting. A pack of M&Ms, peanuts, or an apple around 4:00pm fills out my caloric needs until dinner. But I have used 12:00-1:00pm as a primetime energy burst for me. And, I do not mean to sound judgmental here, if eating at 12:00-1:00pm is something you look forward to and it lifts you up for the rest of the day, then do it. Or, maybe you really like getting out with some friendly coworkers at lunch time. For prime people persons (vs. task junkies), this sounds like an energy burst. Schedule it, keep it, and get energized by it.

Once I get into the office, I will review my emails for any really important developments requiring my immediate attention. Otherwise, if it is a coworker whom I am likely to see during the day, I do not respond. I ask them about it when I see them. If somebody says to the effect, "Did you read the email I sent you?" I respond, "No, but since you mentioned it, tell me all about it." I then have a rich, live person-to-person discussion, save time, and I can usually delete a string of about five related emails at the end of the day without reading them.

I scan headers of emails around midday and again at end of day. I often turn my email system off and do not look at them until the last hour of the day. At that point, I have achieved my agenda. It dawned on me that, if I am traveling or in an all-day meeting, I do not see my emails for 8 or more hours at a time and the world does not crash down. Emails are the biggest threat to productivity nowadays. You must develop disciplines to not let all this electronic chatter hogtie you. Stay on vision. Focus on the big. Drive your energy bursts.

DELEGATE OR DISINTEGRATE

There is a great story in the Bible about one of my favorite leadership heroes, Moses (read Exodus 18:13-29). Early on in Moses' leadership journey, he is drowning in responsibilities. All power is centralized in him and everyone wants to see Moses. The people stand in line from early morning to sundown. Moses is drained by the end of the day and he never gets to his grander vision work. (This was the forerunner of email!) He bemoans all of this to his father-in-law, Jethro, who gives Moses great advice.

Jethro tells Moses, "You can't do this all by yourself, boy. You need to delegate. You've got all these lieutenants working for you, disperse most of your work out to them. These are good people. Give them authority to make decisions. This will free you up for the important work that only you can do." This was great advice from one wise man to another several thousand years ago and it is still sound advice today. Borrowing an insight from Moses experience, remember it is delegate or disintegrate!

DELEGATE TO ACCELERATE
Not only does delegating remove a negative, i.e. the risk that you will wear out like a ten-year-old car. Delegating also has many other positive aspects that accelerate matters. By delegating, you move faster in pursuit of your personal goals and in furthering your significant organizational goals. Also, the more you delegate, the better your people get and the more you can delegate to them because they accelerate their learning. The day goes by a lot faster with less drag because everybody is working on something challenging. There is more energy all around.

Initially in my leadership development, I had difficulty delegating because I suffered from the fear factor that it might not get done right. Or that only I could do it right. Or it will take me more time to explain to somebody else than do it myself. But I had bosses who pushed me hard on this– "Cordivari! You've got to delegate! You cannot do it all by yourself. That is why you have a team!" Over time, I got the message. My team, though junior to me in experience, overall were better experts in sub-areas and came up with creative ways to tackle problems I would never think of. I came to enjoy the surprise of how others came up with solutions through different approaches. This accelerated my learning.

Fast forward to today and I am known as a delegation monster. Whether or not it is at work where I have hundreds of people under my responsibility or at church committee where it is a handful of people, I "delegate to the max," which is my own mental mantra. The personal principles around delegating that I have developed over the years include:

- o If someone else can do it, then I make sure they do it.

- I want to work 100% on only those important tasks that only I can do. I do not want to do any tasks anyone on my team can do.

- I push it down and exhort my direct reports to push it down. When they complain that they cannot push it down anymore, I then ask them to give me one sheet of paper with everything that they or their subordinates are working on. Just show me topics of projects and have their people do the same. I then reset their priorities.

- But I keep the work flowing down and out in pursuit of my goal: I want to work 100% on only those important tasks that only I can do.

- I actually look forward to making the time to explain how to do something new or of a stretch to a subordinate. If you have hired the right kind of people, learning new things and being entrusted with responsibility is energizing. And, I sincerely tell them to drop in if things become unclear at any point.

- But they will complete the task; it is not coming back to me. This all takes some working out but it is a major career and grander vision-maker. You can accomplish nothing of significance if you are mired in minutiae all the time. Delegate to accelerate!

A few parting thoughts on delegation.

- One, in areas of direct and primary responsibility, do not delegate what you do not understand yourself. If you do not know marketing 101, then do not delegate it. Learn it yourself. Once you are an expert, then delegate. Otherwise, you are setting up for disaster.

- Two, you must follow up on what you delegated. You have to have a firm deadline and deliverable with your subordinate. This is how you do personal quality control. Delegate does not mean just forget about it.

Sometimes you do have to delegate what you do not understand where your area of responsibility includes functional areas where you lack in-depth experience. You obviously cannot stop the operation for a year until you become an expert, so you have to delegate and trust. But there are some ways you can keep in control even when leading by delegating in unknown areas.

- Get clear on goals and objectives; how they are measured and how they connect to vision and mission. Does it make sense?

- What are the critical deadlines and deliverables? Get crisp here.

- Who are the key people and processes? Learn these.

- Sit through review questions and ask a lot of common sense questions. Are you getting good answers and is the functional area performing up to expectations.

These are some how-to's on leading in areas where it is not your functional expertise but you are responsible and as leader ultimately accountable.

CREATING AND PRESERVING MONEY

WHAT IS MONEY?

Money is a medium of exchange used by people to trade in the output of their goods and services. This is a fairly formalistic definition of money somewhat etched in my mind from an economics class, let's just say, a long time ago. But it continues to have profound influences on the way I view money for better or worse. If money is a medium of exchange between people, then it is a scorecard. If I am a farmer and I give you a loaf of bread and you are a farmer and you give me a quart of milk in exchange, my measurable score is 1:1. If my bread becomes so good and demand outpaces supply and now you are willing to give me two quarts of milk in exchange for one loaf of bread, my measurable score becomes 2:1.

So, the above example is based on a primitive agrarian economy. Now let us fast forward to the western world in the 21st century of the knowledge economy. There are various ways I can spend my time and the world will give me a measurable exchange for each. If I want to apply my experiences as an executive in the healthcare sector, the world says, "we will pay you $100-$200 an hour and upwards." As a writer, the world says, "we think you are worth about $20 per hour today." And, as a church leader, my value is somewhere between zero and priceless.

So now go back and reflect on the first sentence of this section. *Money is a medium of exchange used by people to trade in the output of their goods and services.* That is pure economics. But it can also become the center of the personal storm brewing inside people who begin to then wrestle with how to spend time. Do you spend your time where the world values your time, or do you spend it where you feel an inner pull, calling and passion? At this juncture, money is now the cornerstone statement of a major life conflict.

Now back to the question again – what is money? Definition number two comes from Tony Robbins, the author, speaker, and personal development guru who defines money along the lines of, "crumpled dirty pieces of paper with the faces of dead people on it." In other words, get beyond the medium of exchange, get beyond the concept of measurable exchange, and then you have a chance to liberate yourself from the $200 per hour versus $20 per hour versus zero/priceless dollars per hour construct above.

SOURCES OF MONEY

You come into the world dumb and naked. At some point, you become self-aware, clothed, cumulating knowledge, and figure out the lines from the old song "money makes the world go 'round."

You need some money. Soon, you figure out that you need "mo' money." What are the sources of money? Over the course of your lifetime, you figure out that there are multiple (legal) sources of money. In some apparent order, the sources are:

- Born with an inheritance. No worries man. (Not!)
- Your parents provide your money.

- Your parents give you an allowance.
- You get your first rudimentary job.
- You elevate to more advanced rudimentary jobs while getting an education.
- After an education of whatever length, you are ready to begin working or procuring money for the rest of your entire life on this planet.
- Cash salary
- Cash bonus
- Stocks and stock options.
- Bonds.
- Deferred income creations.
- Benefits with imputed income
- Interest and dividends from investments
- Gifts from friends and families
- Loans from friends and families
- Loans from banks
- Seed money and serious money from venture capitalists with serious payback expectations
- Angels (wealthy individuals)
- Corporations supporting a cause
- Non-profit organizations and foundations
- Pensions
- Cashed in value of life insurance policies
- Royalties from intellectual property (patents, trademarks, copyrights)
- Rents from real estate
- Plus a hundred other creative instruments that financial institutions and insurance companies dream up continuously

Then when you die, the payout from your life insurance policy and the carve- up of your estate minus taxes starts this cascade all over again for the next generation.

BEGGING FOR MONEY

The words of a country music tune resonate to the effect, I've been rich and I've been poor and I like rich a whole lot more.

It takes money to do almost anything. As previously mentioned, money is somewhere between a medium of exchange between producers of goods and services per Economics 101. Or, money is just pieces of crumpled paper with the pictures of dead people on them.

Work hard for the money. And, along the way, learn to beg, plead, cajole, and/or respectfully inquire for more money from your boss, bank, venture group, corporate overlord, parents, financial angel, church, synagogue, or congregation. And work real hard and smart at whatever you do. If you weren't born a Rockefeller or Kennedy, you must learn to beg for money. The vast majority of human beings will be at somebody's indebtedness for the rest of their lives so we all might as well get used to it.

I know plenty of people in their 60's, all who have been working over 40 years and they are still begging for the money. Examples include an executive negotiating an employment contract, a CEO procuring venture money, a non-profit on a fund-raising drive, the senior minister looking for the new roof for his church. They are all still begging for the money after all these years. That is the bad news. But, I would make the assumption that they have all gotten pretty good at begging for the money after all these years of experience. Start getting good at begging for the money. It is a lifetime practice.

SECURING AND PRESERVING MONEY

Once you have secured money whether in an instant as per loan or gift, or if it is money that has been accumulated over time, you want to quickly re-evaluate your plans of how you intend to spend or disburse it. Now, after all the hard work and begging has been successful, the money is real and mistakes can make it evaporate as quickly as it materialized.

What's the plan, the budget, the expected outcome? Connect the dots from present to future. Will spending the money as you plan drive the outcome you intend and move you closer along the path to your Grander Vision?

Go away, close the door, shut out the world. Find some quiet think time and sort this out. Now that you have secured money, how will you preserve it?

THOUGHTS ON PRESERVING MONEY:
Spend less then you make!

John Templeton, one of the wealthiest and most successful investors of our time, gave these words of advice about how to achieve financial security: "to be financially secure… spend less then you make." Thank you.

Be brutally honest. In *The Laws of Money, The Lessons of Life*, Suze Orman, author and TV celebrity on the subject of you and your money, has as her #1 law: "Truth creates Money, Lies Destroy It." The take-away of the lesson is you must be brutally honest and realistic about money; how much you make, how much you spend.

I carry around this visual in my head that we should all treat money like you would treat blood and bullets. What am I talking about with blood and bullets? The average human being has five quarts of blood in their body. If you are bleeding, you had better put a tourniquet on it or you will be dead fairly shortly.

If you are a soldier in combat under attack and you have only a hundred bullets, you better make your shots count or you will likely be dead shortly.

Make your spending of precious dollars count or you will be financially dead in short order. You will have no medium of exchange (and no crumpled pictures of dead people's faces!).

If you have $10,000 or $10,000,000 in your budget, you'd better make every expenditure count because it will be very difficult to secure more dollars if you have not been a wise steward. The proof of a wise steward is producing results, showing growth, keeping commitments, and achieving timely milestones. Delivering on your financial commitments is currency and credibility in the business world (as well as the non-profit sector!).

MY LITTLE BLUE CHECKBOOK
Spend business money like you are writing a personal check. Over the years, I have been entrusted with increasing financial responsibility in a business. By that, I mean I have larger amounts

of budgets and expenses flowing through my hands, for which I am a steward, am accountable and expected to do really good things with this money to achieve organizational goals. In the crush of a business day, it is easy to get mentally lazy about signing off on invoices, expenses, and budget items that cross my desk. It is millions of dollars we are talking about. It is somebody else's millions of dollars. It came from customers who extracted it from somebody else. Our shareholders expect a profit out of it at the end when all is said and done. But the fact that it is SOMEBODY else's money can make you casual about it. To counteract this negative force, I have developed the following approach which gives me a really finely-honed edge with managing someone else's money.

I pretend that it is MY money and all these expenditures are getting paid out of my little blue checkbook at home. In this scenario, I get to keep the money for myself or write personal checks and give the money away to somebody else. Keep it or give it? Keep it or give it? This visual and mental image gives me a much more robust sense of judgment as a steward of somebody else's money.

In my formative years, I worked for a very successful executive who was the biggest pain in the backside when it came to expenses, budgets, and how you spent the department's money. He would drive us crazy and leave us to mumbling behind his back, saying things like, "You know he acts like this is his own money, what a jerk." Years later, I have learned that this is the only way to be a wise steward of money that is NOT yours, but has been entrusted to you. This former boss of mine got promoted four times in 15 years and now runs a large venture capital fund. He was always wise with money and he was continually rewarded for his money and business judgments.

A HEALTHY VIEW OF MONEY

At one of the Willow Creek Leadership Summits, I heard Rick DeVos speak. Rick is one of the co-founders of Amway and an owner of the Orlando Magic basketball team. He and his wife, Helen, are committed Christians and financially support many kingdom causes. One of the many impressions that Rick left on me was what struck me as his very healthy and balanced view about money. Among the more notable included:

- it is OK to make an enormous amount of money. If you are blessed with a hard work ethic and you work your tail off and you make a bundle of money, you should feel good about it. Unfortunately, the media and most religious leaders seem to communicate otherwise.

- Religious leaders should not put down wealth 51 weeks a year and then come begging to the wealthy that 52nd week which is stewardship Sunday. Show a little appreciation for those who like to work hard and get rewarded for it. (The Bible says that "the love of money is the root of all evil." It does not say that money is the root of all evil.)

-There is no virtue in laziness or under-achievement and society is filled with these types which again the media glorify as victims.

-Give away the first 10% of your money to charitable organizations. He does this and educates all his employees that they should do this. Tithing is not only biblical but it creates a healthy relationship with money.

My take-away from listening to Rick: work hard, make a lot of money, give at least 10% away, and don't feel guilty about your success. It is a very refreshing viewpoint.

HONESTY VERSUS DENIAL IN THE DYNAMICS OF MONEY

As a youngster, I wasn't sure I believed in denial. I heard it existed, but I thought surely people would not want to embrace denial versus grasping reality. But with each passing year, I come to have a great appreciation of the role of denial in the psyche of the human experience. It is almost a universal occurrence and it is never pleasant when reality ultimately comes crashing. You are going to die. Your checkbook is empty. You are fat with those extra 20 pounds. You do not have enough time or resources left to pull off this venture. Get honest. Get real. NOW!

THE WINNERS REALIZE THAT ALL VICTORIES ARE WON ON THE MARGIN AND THEREFORE DON'T GIVE A DIME AWAY TO COMPETITION

I got my MBA from Widener University almost 30 years ago which I say not to impress you or to depress me, but to make a point. It was a great education with most of it buried in my subconscience, producing what I like to call "unconscious competence." But three pieces of learning are still buried in my conscious competence. These are:

1. Look for market research insights that scream, not whisper!
2. Do not hold somebody accountable for an outcome over which they have little control
3. All key business decisions are made on the margin

The first two are fairly self-explanatory but what does the third one mean, you might ask? It means the following when it comes to money and financial commitments:

- The last dollars are the hardest. And victory is defined by the last dollars.
- If forecast if 100, getting to 95 is fairly routine. Finding the last 5 is brutal!
- Amidst all the talk of teamwork, you are advised to fight with all your resolve to hang onto your resources. I am sorry to say that my experience has been, whether in corporations or in church, people rarely remember what a wonderful, loyal selfless team player you were if you give back resources and your team fails to deliver expected results. This may sound a little harsh but I am telling it like it is. Remember, you are marshalling scarce resources!

In the end, yet another measure of your leadership is how effective and compelling you are in arguing the benefit you will produce with the scarce resources given you. So, do not be bashful about seeking time, money, people, and capital. But then be a diligent steward with those resources.

Questions For Reflection:

1. How am I doing on planning my day around the four most critical must do's that will move me along the path to a grander vision achievement? Am I using my daily time on visionary activities or am I being swept along and consumed by the urgent trivialities? Worst yet, am I just going with the flow of whatever pops into the email inbox?

2. In planning my week, can I identify ahead opportunities for "energy bursts" and program them into the week as top priorities?

3. How am I doing at delegating? What are the forces holding me back?

4. What is my relationship with money– healthy or unhealthy? Is it a medium of exchange or a scoreboard for comparison and covetousness? Has it reached the extreme of a "false idol?"

5. Am I being a just steward of all the resources God has put at my disposal?

Prayer

Dear God, please give me the inspiration required that I be a diligent steward of all the resources with which I have been blessed. Everything comes from you. Everything starts with you. I am merely borrowing what you have provided– time, team, money, and talent. Give me the wisdom and the strength to use these to the fullest. Particularly, Lord, when it comes to time, that most fleeting of all resources, let me use to your utmost and with your inspiration. Amen.

Meditation Verse: Ecclesiastes 3:1
"There is a time for everything and a season for every activity under heaven."

CHAPTER 7

Execute The Vision

"Dreams without action are just fantasies."
 - Bob Rotella

"All line managers hear this: execute...or be executed!"
 - Anonymous former boss

EXECUTION: THE WILL TO GET IT DONE

Execution could be described in its simplest term as 'the state of getting it done.' It is the state of realizing forecasted visions, goals, and objectives. It is walking the talk. One of the primary characteristics of leaders who can execute is a personal and intense commitment to get it done.

While I have never met Jack Welch, the former CEO of General Electric, it was widely alleged that his ability to get things done through the sheer power of his will– and execute– is what made him one of the most successful CEOs of the 20th century. At Johnson and Johnson, Ralph Larsen and his successor as CEO, Bill Weldon, both had this power of presence as did Vice-Chairman, Bob Wilson. These gentlemen were my senior executives during most of my career at J&J.

The world of sports has a lot of similar analogies. Michael Jordan will be remembered certainly as a very gifted basketball player. But it was his burning desire to win and to "get it done" which made him most formidable. It was the combination of his gifts, commitment to practice, and willpower to win, or execute, that made Michael Jordan one of the greatest athletes ever.

Whether the stories come from the realm of business, sports, or the military, the message is the same. In a phrase, execution means: Getting IT done!

AND TO INSTALL THE SAME BELIEF IN YOUR TEAM
If you demonstrate the ethos described above as a leader, you have once again secured the high ground and the ability to lead by your example. Communicate that we are not in this to just compete, to try, to attempt, or to just give our best effort. Don't get too carried away with the viewpoint of "let's just enjoy the journey." No, communicate that you expect unambiguous victory, unconditional surrender, the BIG win. Establish a culture that you expect commitment to goals, objectives, and deliverables. Commitment equals credibility and credibility is critical when you depend on outsiders for continuous resources over the long run.

HIRE OR TRAIN OR SANITIZE TO WIN
The best ways to ensure successful execution is first of all to hire, train, or sanitize your team so you have a group that all internally share a passion at winning, no matter what the endeavor. From this starting point, an execution mode is internally driven and you do not need be a continuous trail boss in order to get things done; done well, and done well on time.

You also need to be mentally and emotionally tough enough to remove, make changes, and/or take action against any team members who have lost credibility with you by their repeated failure to execute and deliver on their commitments. A chain is only as strong as the weakest link, and so it goes with execution. Be kind, be fair, but be firm and resolute. The entire venture is at stake.

INSPIRE THE HEARTS AND MANAGE THE TASKS
So much of execution is task management, planning, problem anticipation, problem solving, and mid-course corrections. It is the stuff of project management, follow-up, and regular performance reviews. <u>It is about the right things getting done well and on time.</u>

But is it also about inspiring the hearts of your teammates so they will be positively motivated to operate at this very high level and the personal intensity required. Constantly energize them, say thank you, show gratitude, catch them doing things right, celebrate small wins, and release the tension when it nears toxic levels.

EXECUTION REQUIRES THE RIGHT PEOPLE, STRATEGY AND RESOURCES

If you have not yet done so, I encourage you to read one of the more definitive works on the subject of execution. In the bestseller entitled, *Execution*, authors Larry Bossidy (former Chairman of Honeywell International) and Ram Charan (renowned management consultant) put forth a persuasive case from first-hand experiences with many large organizations that execution requires three critical ingredients:

1. The right people
2. Who can execute the chosen strategy
3. Provided with the proper resources.

The BIGGER the goal or the vision, then the more important it is to get these three things right: sharper people in key positions, clearer focus of strategy, critical mass of resources. The important point I want to make here is that, while the aforementioned willpower of the leader to "get it done" is critical, that is not enough on its own. Or, as my friend and long-standing management consultant, Dr. Edwin Glasscock, likes to say, "necessary but not sufficient." In addition to the leader's innate power, it is necessary to staff the team with the right people, choose the right strategy, and get them the adequate resources they need to be successful.

When you feel challenged to pray about your business, there are few areas that are more important and in need of some "divine providence" from the senior partner up above. There is nothing wrong with asking God's help in hiring decisions, strategic choices, or in your allocation of scarce resources. These are critical ingredients for execution. Why would you, as a fallible human, try to take on these massive decisions and judgments alone?

MAKE THE BIG MANAGEABLE

TAKE THE GRAND VISION AND CHOP IT UP INTO MANAGEABLE PIECES.

I have been associated with significant ventures both in our local church and in the corporate world. We have run a couple of capital campaigns to expand our physical property and buildings at our church. These campaigns were usually two years in the planning and three years in the "doing."

In the corporate world, I have worked with numerous new product development and launch programs. It takes a good seven years to take a pharmaceutical agent from early research through development and then successful market entry. My involvement was from the business perspective, but always working closely with the R&D team.

Whether it was the corporate or church world, there were hundreds of major tasks to get done; get done well and on time. In both realms, they involved the pursuit of what Jim Collins, author of best-sellers *Built to Last* and *Good to Great* termed BHAGs which stands for...Big Hairy Audacious Goals. These were ventures with big stakes, huge risks, and long horizons. In one venture, we were saving lives and in the other we were saving souls. You don't manage, lead, or run ventures of this scope or magnitude on the back of an envelope. You need to organize, in a very orderly process, a lot of "sub-contracts" to make it happen.

CHOP THE GRAND VISION INTO MANAGEABLE BITES OF TIME, RESOURCES AND PEOPLE DELIVERABLES

Take a five-year plan and see the whole picture by way of large pieces of paper taped together across your desk or on the wall. Write it out by hand. (There's that darn "writing" command again.)

Chop the 5 years into one-year blocks; segment the years into quarters and then into months. Chop the finished product (i.e. think as though it was a car) into major meaningful groupings – engine, drive-frame, chassis, body, controls, tires, all other.

Determine how much time, people, and money of your limited budget is required to pull all this off. It's not that hard. It looks massive. It's not. It's as easy as putting a puzzle together. It just takes commitment, time, and persistence on your part as the leader.

I have read stories about CEOs who planned large acquisitions this way. Before they get all the staffs and technology wizards involved, who will figure things out to eight decimal places, they just need to see the whole big picture themselves. This allows them to line things up in their gut as well as strengthening their ability to lead the organization on this massive high-risk task.

DELEGATE! ASSIGN AN ACCOUNTABLE OWNER TO EACH PIECE AND TEACH ACCOUNTABILITY

Then go through the plan with your team in mind and, either by yourself or with your subordinates, come up with the most appropriate and capable person for each task. It is usually best if you choose the accountable owner for the broad categories (engine, drive-frame, chassis, etc.) and then let them decide who should be on their team that would be best for the sub-tasks. This is delegation, empowerment, ownership, and pushing decisions down closer to the people with the most useful information. They also have the best grasp of reality and the expertise to get it done.

THE LEADER'S FOCUS FOR EXECUTING

LIST ALL PROJECTS THAT NEED TO BE MANAGED AND HAVE AN ACCOUNTABLE OWNER FOR EACH

There are few things that cause paralysis of progress, like being mentally swamped. You are in the mental swamp when you catch yourself thinking, "I've got so much to do. I don't know where to start." Counterattack. You want to get out of here quickly. Antidote to escape the mental swamp: List all, and I mean all; whether ten, a hundred, or a thousand tasks, and ensure that you have an accountable owner for each. If not, this is your First Things First priority as leader.

AS LEADER, FOCUS YOUR TIME, TALENT, ENERGY AND RESOURCES ON THE TOP 10 PROJECTS

Now you have a fence around all the projects. They are all on paper and not rattling around in your head anymore. Now do some critical thinking. With your team, decide what are the Top 10 most critical projects that will result in a "sink or swim" outcome for the Vision. These are the 10 you want on your radar screen. The success of the venture and your accountability as the leader depends upon them.

DO NOT OWN THESE PROJECTS; BE THE OVERLORD

One of the critical laws of high performance managers is that they do NOTHING that someone else is capable of. They focus on spending their time on things that only they can do. This practice results in productivity, leverage, acceleration and personal growth.

Be clear to yourself so you can be clear to your team: you do not own the execution of these projects, one of your team members does. But you are going to add value by infusion of sharing best management practices, leadership principles, and raising the probability of success by elevating visibility. You are the sponsor or overlord.

INSPECT, EXPECT, RESPECT

There is a relationship across the concepts of *inspect, expect, respect*. What you inspect, people will see as something you expect, which in turn makes them respect the importance of the activity. As a sales manager, I wanted my team making eight calls a day, which was the industry average at the time. By constantly calling attention to the weekly activity report, people knew that I would inspect their productivity; I expected eight calls per day, and they respected that they were going to have to make an accounting in this area.

What you inspect, people will come to expect and you will have their respect for the task or activity.

MANAGE THE REMAINING PROJECTS ON AN EXCEPTION BASIS.

Manage the remaining 80% of the projects which probably account for 40% or less of the value on an exception basis. On a monthly basis, you want to know which projects are seriously behind their timeline or over budget. And while the converse is rare, you also want to know which are ahead of forecast and under-spent (wonderful but rare!).

NEVER STOP ASKING WHO WILL DO WHAT BY WHEN

DO NOT BELIEVE ANYTHING WILL GET DONE UNTIL YOU HAVE IN WRITING <u>WHO</u> WILL DO <u>WHAT</u> BY <u>WHEN</u>.

Eric Milledge is a senior executive at Johnson and Johnson and was one of the most effective and inspirational bosses I ever worked for. Eric is and was a people person, had high standards, focused on results, and was a motivational leader.

Eric also had a unique way of deflecting a decision he did not want to make and he was also very adept at rejecting your proposal without making you feel rejected. The drill would go something like this. Through his executive antennae, if he was going to give you sixty minutes of his time then he wanted to know ahead of time why you were *really* meeting with him. The sixty-minute meeting would then go something like this: the first twenty-five minutes, he would tell you all about his weekend or some interesting world potentate he had just met. He is a very good storyteller. The next twenty-five minutes, he wanted to hear all about your life, job, and organization. The last ten minutes, he would hear the highlights of your proposal, tell you why it had some merit but what more was required to get him to fully support it. After such a meeting, people would frequently comment something to the effect, "He said 'no,' but he makes you feel good just spending time with him."

I share the anecdote above to emphasize what a great touch Eric has with people. And, to reinforce the point that, in addition to being a great people person, Eric is an incredibly effective taskmaster and executor. He imbedded in me the following corollary, which has become a foundation for me regarding execution:

" If it isn't on paper with somebody's name beside a deliverable by a hard date, then I have no confidence it will get done."

I found out the hard way over the years that he is and was right, and I now have long lived by this corollary. Make it work for you.

THE SEVEN QUESTIONS YOU SHOULD CONTINUOUSLY ASK

The seven questions that you, as leader, should continuously ask are: who, what, where, when, why, how, and how much?

<u>Who</u> is going to do it, get it done, and be held accountable?

<u>What</u> is the deliverable? Are we clear on both sides?

<u>Where</u> will you get resources or from what other project will you steal the time to do it?

<u>When</u> will it be delivered? We are talking commitment here.

<u>Why</u> are we doing it? How does it connect to Vision, strategy, and results?

<u>How</u> will it get done? What's the total plan? What is fantasy vs. reality?

<u>How Much</u> will is cost? Whose budget is carrying the cost? What is the source of the funding?

THE POWER OF THE REVIEW SESSIONS

WEEKLY REVIEWS ("KNOW WHO'S GOT THE MONKEY")

Weekly reviews should be *your* reviews. They are *your* list of nagging details, thorny issues; yellow flags you fear may become red flags. Make them informal. Drop-in. Set up a pre-scheduled teleconference call if one party is traveling. Email is OK but weak and leaving a voicemail is really weak.

The preferred media for your weekly reviews are in order of preference: a live drop in, a scheduled 10 minutes, or a scheduled phone call. Caveat: As you uncover thorny issues in your weekly reviews, do not let these issues become your issues to solve. In the words of a classic Harvard Business Review article (Onchen and Wass, 11/1/1999), "Who's Got the Monkey?"
(Answer: The manager does not have the monkey; the subordinate does.)

MONTHLY REVIEWS

Monthly reviews should be "sit downs" lasting 1 to 1 ½ hours with you and the accountable owner and perhaps one to three other members of the team who are steeped in the details.

At Johnson & Johnson, the ethos was: keep the participants to a minimum. The expectation was that the accountable owner would own the project and be able to address all issues. This was also effective management developing training, forcing you to get down into key details. Also, the boss wanted to be free to speak his or her mind as the situation dictated and they could be more open, the less people were in the room. They did not like to be perceived as putting you down in front of your people.

(P.S. It is very bad form to dress down a leader in front of their team. You will totally undermine their authority, empowerment, and the respect of the team. If you support them, then support them 100%. And if you do not, then start taking actions to remove them. But do not demean them in public and/ or in front of their team.)

QUARTERLY REVIEWS

Quarterly reviews are half-day reviews with the accountable leader and their subordinates parading through with select details as needed. The quarterly review should start with you and the accountable owner to get all the ground rules and background posturing cleared up.

Then, bring all the contributors in. The advantage is that you get to hear all the details first hand. You also get to observe the second tier of personnel and decide if you see any early rising stars for the future. You get to imprint your leadership messages further down the organization.

When the meeting is over, give the group some feedback and closure on accomplishments and shortfalls. Be clear on next steps and owners. You are mentoring execution in this manner.

Finish up the review with a short one-on-one with the accountable owner. This is where you can be as frank and as blunt as you want without the person's team being witness to it. You support your leaders in public – their job is tough enough. You give coaching, mentoring, feedback, counseling in a one-on-one personal setting.

ANNUAL REVIEWS

Annual reviews are all day reviews, best done in January or February if December 31 is the close of final results. If a major project, like a new product launch or major advertising campaign ends in, say, May – then do the full annual all-day review in June or July while everything is still fresh. You want to be able to give full and meaningful feedback so be sure the final, final results are in. A 99 is a failure on a commitment of 100. September 1 is failure on a commitment of August 31.

The format or agenda of an annual review should be:

- Final results vs. plan or intent
- Reasons to celebrate (+) or commiserate (-)
- Lessons learned (allow acceptance that things go wrong)
- On a 1-10 scale, how would you and the team rate performance
- Give overall feedback and leave the team with one or two major things to focus on for improvement. But also, and most important, reinforce the strengths that they should continue to exploit to the fullest as they move forward.

ONLY THE PARANOID SURVIVE (OR...ANOTHER SLEEPLESS NIGHT)

There is nothing wrong with a sleepless night that is fueled by the excitement of wanting to solve a breakthrough problem and you just cannot turn your inquisitive mind to the off mode. But there is a difference between that situation and one who lies in bed awake at 3:00am worrying themselves sick about endless little problems. I used to be one of these people. I came to refer to the phenomena as "my rolodex" of worries. I could have twenty things I was worrying about and spend 10-15 minutes on one; think I solved it for now; move on to number two; repeat, EXHAUSTING!

When I married Cyndee, there became quite a contrast in our sleep patterns. She would sleep uninterrupted for eight straight hours and wake up looking so refreshed. I asked that she tell me her secret. She shared with me that I was to give up each day to God at the end of the day and to ask him to help solve my problems tomorrow. And, in between, to ask for a good night's sleep. This may sound simple or unbelievable to you, but I found it revolutionary and transformational. On the whole, I have slept very well since having this wisdom imparted to me close to twenty years ago by my loving and wise wife. If you want to become God's leader, then you have to learn to trust God in all areas of your life– including a good night's sleep! On the other hand, there is nothing wrong with having a temporary obsession about a nagging but important detail when, lo and behold, the solution comes to you in a semi-conscious state in the middle of the night. The Bible often speaks of God speaking to his leaders in the form of a dream in the middle of the night. I think he just plants the idea while I am sleeping. How great is that!

So, as you can probably tell, I have a much stronger spiritual platform at this point in my leadership journey. If I happen to wake up at 3:00AM, rather than let the Evil One tangle me up in the rolodex of worries, I take it as an opportunity to connect with the Holy Spirit. I get totally quiet and still before God, and offer up a business or life issue to God and pray something like, "Lord, please help me with this challenge. Place a thought in my mind or heart and let me hear what you are telling me. Let me be guided by your will not mine. I surrender 100% and trust the outcome."

COVER THE DOWNSIDES AND THE UPSIDES WILL TAKE CARE OF THEMSELVES

Every great plan should be thought of in terms of having a base, upside, and downside scenario:

The base case is your very best thinking on what reality ought to be when all things have been considered and you have done all in your power to insure this outcome.

The downside scenario is a look at what happens if some of your assumptions do not materialize, or if events beyond your control occur to rain on your parade. Examples of things beyond your control: a terrorist act dampens consumer optimism.

The upside scenario is what the outcome could be, should you catch a positive break. Example: a more favorable exchange rate against a critical currency due to vast macroeconomic issues beyond your control.

YOU WANT AN EARLY WARNING SYSTEM FOR PROBLEMS.

These are the potential disasters that can sink your venture and crash your Grand Vision. You want to place priority attention at ensuring these don't take place. You need early warning systems for any adverse developments so you can react quickly. You need to have contingency plans in place to anticipate untoward events. It was drilled into me over the years, "If you cover the downsides, the upsides will take care of themselves."

MONOMANIACAL FOCUS ON THE APPROACHING GOAL LINE

People at Boston Scientific say that Jim Tobin, their CEO, constantly preaches the value of a maniacal focus and tells them that he is the company's "chief maniac." I like that. The leader has to *lead* the charge in getting everyone zeroed in on what is critical, what is a priority, and what must get done. And this is particularly true as deadlines for execution and deliverables draw near.

747 PILOT

I love airplanes, particularly big jets. I have been blessed to log millions of miles safely and comfortably all over the world. I appreciate the banter of the pilots with the passengers. Points of attraction out the right side, temperature, elevation, flying time, expected arrival, etc. It is reassuring to hear the leader's voice who is entrusted with the lives of hundreds.

But as you start the final approach, you do not hear from the captain again until we are safely on the ground. He has a monomaniacal focus on getting that expensive plane loaded with fragile life on the ground safely. Focus on the approaching victory like a jumbo jet pilot focused on the approaching runway.

HARBOR PILOT

A large tanker or luxury cruise ship will make a transoceanic voyage of thousands of miles. But as they approach the destination or interim ports of call, they pause before the final approach. They double and triple check harbor maps and await the arrival of the harbor pilot who will guide them in. I was on a cruise recently and watched awestruck at the captain, officers, and harbormasters as we made our final approach. Their intensity and focus was palpable. Focus on the approaching goal line like the ship's captain navigating the threatening rocks and sandbars just prior to achieving their accomplished mission of a safe and damage-free docking at their intended port-of-call.

ARNOLD PALMER AND THE COMPETITIVE EDGE

Arnold Palmer is undisputed as one of the greatest golfers of all time. He has the trophies, the prize money, and the results to establish that claim. The late Mark McCormick, author of *What They Don't Teach You At Harvard Business School* (page 255) relates his insights on what made Arnold Palmer such a successful professional golfer. He cited three necessary behaviors required for the competitive edge necessary to become a champion. They were:

(1) The champion's profound sense of dissatisfaction with their own accomplishments. They use any success, any victory as a spur to greater ambition.

(2) The ability to peak their performances, to get themselves up for major tournaments.

(3) The ability to put their opponents away. This is referred to as "the killer instinct" but that tells you more about the result of what is going on mentally.

McCormick summarizes these behaviors with, "In the champion's mind he is never ahead. He distorts reality to serve his competitive purpose. He is always coming from behind, even when the score indicates he is destroying his opponent. He never believes he is performing as well as he actually is."

I have always remembered this vignette by McCormick on golfers and other championship athletes and translated this in my own mind as it pertains to leadership and execution as the following trio:

(1) Focus on the immediate task at hand and blot out distractions

(2) Do not let your competitor come back when they have faltered

(3) Personally commit to the approaching victory with focus, intensity, and willpower. Never let it slip away!

The lesson from Arnold Palmer and Mark McCormick is that, regardless of your field of endeavor, one must develop the critical skills and behavioral traits of having monomaniacal focus on the approaching victory.

4TH QUARTER – ITS GAME TIME!
I ran a business unit at Johnson and Johnson for much of my career there. I learned that the fourth quarter of the year required an even higher level of focus and intensity. You had to keep a closer look at spends versus budgets, sales versus projections, billings and collections; all to ensure that you brought your numbers in right where you committed they would be. My team and I did this successfully all but one year. That was a painful experience never to be repeated. The lesson learned was: do not over-promise. If you are falling short of your commitments, you must declare the event as soon as possible and take your medicine

versus sugar-coating the situation in October and falling short in December when there is little room for your superiors to put their contingency plan in place.

DONE! MISSION ACCOMPLISHED!

Some visioneers believe that you never say "vision accomplished!" They hold the point-of-view that visions should be so big and lofty that you would likely never fully achieve them. "Conquering outer space" might be a vision and "going to the moon" would be a mission along the way.

So, the vision of whatever your venture is should be so HUGE that it looks impossible. But if it directs you in pursuit of your dreams and allows you "to go to the moon," it plays a vital role as beacon light, energizer, and motivator along the way.

AGAIN...MISSION AND VISION

Many people have a very vague or interchangeable view about mission and vision. It need not be the case. They are two very separate elements that play different roles in maintaining focus.

Mission is the purpose or reason for being of a person or team or large organization. The army gives every unit a mission. The missions are very clear and achievable such as "secure hilltop alpha and eliminate the enemy who stand in the way." Missions should be clear, tangible, and executable in the present.

Vision is the lofty state or BIG audacious hairy grand goal you strive to achieve. Cure world hunger. Make the world safe for democracy. Conquer outer space. It is vast and "out there" on the time horizon.

VICTORY – "IT AIN'T OVER 'TIL IT'S OVER"

The goal line is approaching. It is the end of the project. The fourth quarter is closing. It's the 18th hole. Your manuscript has been accepted for publication. Remember, "it ain't over 'til it's over!"

Focus. "There is many a slip between cup and lip." Don't fumble. Close the books. Sink the putt. See your published book up on the shelf. Then and only then, may you relax, collapse, cry out, claim, and savor your victory because you have learned the discipline of execution which is – "get it done."

Questions For Reflection:

1. As I progress daily to execute against the annual plan and the far-out vision, am I leading (inspiring hearts and souls) and managing (focused on tasks and things) as appropriate for the specific situation?

2. Am I micromanaging (in way too deep or second-guessing after the fact) or delegating (empowering someone for the outcome)?

3. Am I continually asking the right questions of the right people to get an accurate portrayal of reality?

4. Am I spending quality time with key people to review projects but equally important– to relate, to bond, and to truly hear their needs and issues required for them to be successful in their job?

5. Am I monomaniacally focused on the approaching goal line to ensure the final steps in execution?

Prayer

Dear Lord, at the end of the day, vision is a Big Idea. But, sadly, too often the vision lacks execution and fades away as a fantasy. Through the power of the Holy Spirit and your favor which I do not deserve, let me employ all my talents and put unfailing belief in the Lord of the Impossible. Help me successfully execute (and keep me from getting executed!).

Meditation Verse: Proverbs 16:3
"Commit to the Lord whatever you do and your plans will succeed."

CHAPTER 8

Savor Victory; Learn from Defeat

"Failure is not fatal and success is not forever."
 - Don Shula

"Life is not a game of perfect. Accept the outcome."
 - Bob Rotella

SMELL THE ROSES AND PUT THE CELL PHONE DOWN!

I hate cell phones. Yes, on the one hand they could be the greatest technology breakthrough since the wheel, but conversely, cell phones are near temptations of really bad behavior.

Is there anything worse than a boorish person yapping at the top of their lungs in a supermarket, or train, or in a closed-space like an airplane, as though they were the only people in the world?

I personally believe that cell phones are like a Novocain to Type A personalities who dread not having something to do at all times.

STOP THE OIL TANKER

You have been going full-tilt towards the approaching goal line and you sprinted towards the end to ensure the victory. But now it is time to stop. Like an oil tanker in motion at sea, it is not easy to stop a super-achiever and pursuer of grand visions.

But you can stop and relax. Let your pulse slow down and shut down the adrenaline for a brief respite. You can release focus Don't shave. Drop out of sight. Go to a remote location. Get lost in Nordstrom's for a day. Do whatever it takes to chill out. Because...

IT'S DONE. IT'S REALLY DONE.

If you have completed a major project or delivered on an annual plan, then you have achieved a major milestone towards your grander vision. It is hard to register, but it is done. It takes some time for reality to sink in. In the 2003 US Tennis Open, Andy Roddick approached match point with this incredible intensity and focus in his eyes. He was one point away from realizing a lifelong dream. You could see that he was visibly pumped up. In the ensuing moments, he delivered four aces that might have been four of the fastest ever. You only saw the ball hitting the court. The flight path of the serve was a blur. He won. It was done. It took about 5 seconds to settle in. He collapsed to the court overwhelmed with emotion at achieving a grand vision he had crafted way back as a young child. "Andy, it's done, it's really done." You could see the reality of it all sinking in.

TAKE INVENTORY OF YOUR LIFE, CAREER AND ACHIEVEMENTS

Where do you go next? For many its "peat" and repeat; sports jargon for winning the ultimate championship three times. But each repeating win gets harder and delivers less joy, generally speaking, than the preceding win.

Then one day, the Grand Vision starts bordering on drudgery. That's OK. Do not panic. It is just time to start crafting a new Grand Vision. Take inventory of what is really important to you. Time passes and things change. Get introspective, seek solitude, talk to your Creator, and discern the next grand step on the journey.

AND KNOW WHO IS REALLY IN CONTROL

There is a lyric from a popular Christian rock song that frequently comes into my mind. The refrain goes:

> "There is a reason, a time and a season, God is in control."

I know who is in control of my life. When I reflect, I am blown away how circumstances over which I had absolutely zero control had the most significant impact on my life. My parents are the greatest gifts of love a child could ever want. I received this gift free from God. My four brothers and sister are all my best friends and a source of 24/7 unconditional love that I always know I can count on. I obviously had nothing to do with them being placed in my life.

I had been on a thousand airline flights and rarely spoke to the person beside me, preferring a good book instead. One night on a 35-minute flight, I was "randomly" seated next to a complete stranger. On this night I did talk to the special person seated beside me whose name was Cyndee. That "random" event has been the source of so many joys and blessings for me. We have been happily married and together for close to twenty years now. Today, I hardly think there was anything random about our meeting. We have been blessed with wonderful children and have created a loving family. Cyndee introduced me to a Steve McConnell, with whom she had attended college. Steve is the Senior Pastor at Liberty Corner Presbyterian Church. Cyndee and I joined Liberty Corner where I took on leadership positions and grew richly in my faith. Steve opened my world up to Bill Hybels and Willow Creek Community Church and the Willow Creek Leadership Summits. Bill Hybels planted the idea of living a life of a grander vision. Those words became the seedling of the idea that produced this book. Cyndee's sister, Helen, gave me my first readable Bible.

I have Cyndee to thank for my faith, my pastor, my Bible, and the connected dots to the idea for this book. I have Cyndee to thank for our children, for being a totally loving wife, and making my life incredibly joyous. I have God to thank for putting me next to Cyndee on a 35-minute flight. I place my faith in God to control my life. He has done such a superb job and I shutter to think what a mess I make when I try to take matters into my own hands.

It was only recently that it fully dawned on me that the things which had the most significant and positive impact on the outcome of my life and career were the things over which I had absolutely zero control.

On by 50th birthday, I reflected that I was very pleased with how my life had turned out – loving wife, great kids, enriching career, rekindled faith, large and loving family.

And then I realized that I didn't pick my parents or the country where I live and which I love; had nothing to do with my innate intelligence which was genetic; how I met my wife (happenstance); how I got the greatest job ever (serendipity); five children miraculously born 100% healthy, happy, and wonderful; a Savior who died for me to provide me eternal life. These things comprise all the great joys of my life. I had zip, nada, nothing to do with them. All I can say is "Praise the Lord!" I know where to place the glory and I know who is in control of my life.

THE NEW YOU: DON'T SELL YOURSELF SHORT

When I was a 20-something sales rep interviewing with a sales training manager, I thought a person of his position had achieved the unattainable. When I interviewed with his boss the Division Manger, I felt like this person was a minor god. And then I was finally interviewed by the RM (regional sales manager) who impacted me with several impressions: This man is awesome, brilliant, and incredible (and he hadn't even spoke yet). This position is totally out of my reach. I will never in a hundred years become a regional sales manager.

The reality was that I achieved career success many positions higher than RM, but with each successive minor victory, I would immediately minimize the achievement. Not as tough or impressive as I thought, I would reflect.

DON'T GET TOO INFLATED

I would immediately sell myself short and downplay the achievement of a life-long vision or career goal. You can err the other way, too. I still remember the first day on the job when asked to take over as president at Ortho Derm, a Johnson & Johnson business unit.

I thought I was hot stuff. My self-talk and self-image became very pumped up. In the realm of corporate politics, I had vanquished the vanquishers. I had been vindicated. Top Dog moving into the corner office today. There is a New Sheriff in town. As I kissed my wife good-bye that morning, unsolicited, she said, "Honey, don't get a big head. Be nice. Be gracious." You gotta love her.

She picks me up or takes me down a notch whatever the situation requires.

FINDING THE RIGHT BALANCE

So, find the right balance; what some call the center point. Not too hot or too cold. Not too egotistical, not too lacking in self-esteem. You deserve your victory due to your hard work, commitment, dedication, leadership, and management skills.

But there were others; there was a team; there was the luck of timing and place. There was the influence of mentors, teachers, and former bosses. Lastly, don't be too quick to discount destiny and divine providence.

FULLY RECOGNIZE THE CONTRIBUTIONS OF YOUR TEAM

It is a rare and golden opportunity to fully recognize the contributions of your team. I am sure that you have been on many teams as leader or contributor. You know what it is like to hear a thank you. You also know what a slap it is to be overlooked for your contributions.

Do not ever miss the opportunity in the aftermath of victory or achievement as the leader to say, "Thank you. Hey, well done. Bravo. Kudos. I really appreciate your effort and commitment. I couldn't have done it without you." Talk about energy!

PUBLIC ACCLAMATION

And, for a huge leverage effect (remember leverage is one input in; ten outputs out), say all these things in front of other people. Proclaim it. The more important in size and influence the audience is, the more "juice" your statement of gratitude to the individual will carry.

But be sincere. If someone didn't do a great job, don't squander this precious vehicle with cheap pandering. You will send the wrong message and hurt your credibility. And, you will also cheapen the value of this precious and scarce currency. But use the public forum to proclaim contributions of and gratitude towards individuals and the team. Everybody wins and benefits.

PRIVATE ADMONITION

Practice public acclamation but private admonition. I have observed over the years that it is a best practice of top leaders who always display dignity and respect for fellow human beings, regardless of rank or privilege.

If the best thing you can do is publicly show gratitude and appreciation, one of the worst things you can do is "rip" somebody in public. They might deserve it. You might think it will feel good. It is a power flex. But it is a loss all around. The person will be humiliated, think ill of you, spread bad views about you, and likely spend the rest of their days seeking revenge in one way or another.

YOU WILL NEED YOUR TEAM AGAIN. PREPARE THE WAY

It is all right and even desirable to publicly talk with your entire team about what is going well and what is not. But focus on the task or function and don't publicly belittle or put down individuals.

Sanitize or replace them in a professional and efficient way. Thank your team privately and publicly. Show dignity and respect always; you will want them again. And now with a public victory, others are going to want your teammates on their team as well. I mean this whether speaking intramural within an organization, or external to the competitive world at large. You are in a competitive bidding situation. Treat your team well and you can build off success and avoid starting all over again with recruiting and the drag of having empty slots in key positions.

FINDING THE NEXT NEW THING

Let's go back and talk about the oil tanker again. The oil tanker on the high seas that cannot change direction readily is a metaphor of life experience. If it takes that tanker one mile to change direction with the engine off, it seems like it takes us humans many years in our precious life to change direction even though we want to. We get so stuck in our ways either avoiding fears or settling into "successes". And there are many forces that make it difficult to change direction even when we badly want to.

LAUNCH OFF THE <u>NEW</u> YOU AND NOT THE <u>OLD</u> YOU
At one point in my career, I fell in love with my business card and stayed in a job long after the joy was gone. The card contained three data points I absolutely loved and was perversely attached to. These were:
- My name: Me. It is all about me, right? (Wrong)
- My title. Company president
- And best of all the beautiful red script in the corner that read "A Johnson & Johnson Company"

These three lines on the card had all blurred and merged into the definition of who I was. A new me had been born over the course of the decade I was in this job but I was oblivious to it for too long. I had gotten stuck mentally, emotionally, spiritually and physically between the old me and the new me.

GO BOUNDARYLESS
I loved my career at Johnson & Johnson. Twenty-two exciting, wonderful, growth, and learning-filled years. The association with excellent people– bosses, top executives, teammates – was just an absolute gift. I didn't just drag myself off to work every day. I went to a factory that took willing individuals and molded them into world-class leaders, managers, and human beings.

But I woke up one day and knew I had outgrown it. It was time for something way bigger. J&J had prepared me for it. I believe I was called from my job by God without the next assignment being clear. It was scary and exhilarating. But I was ready to go "boundaryless" and trust in God for my next really exciting assignment.

"DON'T SETTLE FOR PERCH"
The words of Bill Hybels continued to ring in my ears: "Don't settle for perch." We talked about this previously. This is what, in so many words, Jesus spoke when he called Peter and Andrew.

Don't settle for perch, you fisherman. Come and become fishers of men. Become part of an eternal movement that has persisted 2,000+ years and will never die.

During this season of change in my life and my career, I entertained scores of career opportunities across the full panorama of big and small company, profit and non-profit, self-employed and consulting. One of these opportunities is noteworthy to recount. I came so close to accepting a position with a small Christian non-profit organization in Lititz, Pennsylvania whose only product was distributing Bible tracts. Lititz is this peaceful rural hamlet about two hours west of Philadelphia. The name of the organization is The Pocket Testament. I had three interviews with the CEO, Mike Brickley. I did not know if God was calling me or what inner voice I was listening to. Jesus says that you must be ready to leave all behind and pick up my cross and come follow me. I believe that. There was a "but" with Lititz. We were not ready to move from our cozy spot in New Jersey to the rural country of Pennsylvania. Nor uproot our kids from their schools and leave their friends behind. Oh, yes, and one more thing. I was not ready to take a 75% pay cut from what I had become accustomed to and for what I believe I needed to support a young family while I was approaching "senior citizen" status. I do not know if I walked away from God's calling at that time. My wife and I prayed intensely. I must admit that the parable about the rich man who could not walk away from his earthly trappings to follow Jesus echoed in my bones for a long time (see Matthew 19:16-22).

But if I was going to walk away from this, I knew the next position had to be HUGE in terms of purpose. I prayed to God to the effect of, "Dear Lord, I am not ready to go to Lititz. I hope I am not disappointing you. I hope I am not turning my back on a special assignment. I hope this was just part of the journey. I do want to take a step up and employ all the skills I have developed over the last thirty years to do something huge for humanity."

In the next part of this saga, I had a networking breakfast meeting with Grant Bogle, a friend from church. His wife and my wife were members of the same Bible study small group from church. Grant was in the midst of being downsized and looking at a lot of opportunities. He told me about a small company nearby that he felt would be of high interest to me given what I was looking for. He was right. I felt an immediate connection to INO Therapeutics in Clinton, New Jersey.

INO is what is known in the pharmaceutical industry as an "orphan drug company." Orphan drugs are those pharmaceutical products wherein the market is so small as to make the vast development undertaking and financial risk untenable for anyone with "common sense." So, there had to be a vehicle for injecting uncommon sense into a situation where there is a pressing human need that exceeds financial common sense. To this problem, the government came up with the solution of "orphan drug" designation. This gives the investors some years of marketplace exclusivity and some tax breaks. But they are still very tiny and underserved markets in the grand schemes of billion dollar corporations.

So, I discovered INO Therapeutics and hit it off with the founders and the new CEO, Dennis Smith. He and the recruiters said "come up and talk and see if we can't come up with something of interest to you." In short I said, "I have done sales, marketing, international, business development and general management over the course of my career." So, Dennis said, "Great. Why don't you run sales, marketing, business development and our emerging international business?" It sounded exciting and I accepted.

INO Therapeutics has been a wonderful experience working in the critical care arena. Our lead product is a pharmaceutical in the form of a gas that is used to help rescue babies born in respiratory distress and with breathing problems. I had totally enjoyed my last assignment at Johnson and Johnson as company president of a dermatological business, but I was yearning for something bigger and not just in terms of "moving up the corporate ladder." The next assignment was saving babies. This was big. This was huge.

HOW TO TAKE A REAL VACATION

But before I switched jobs, I did what I strongly encourage you to do in this situation. Take a vacation to clear your head and start on a refreshed clean slate. At Johnson and Johnson, I also learned how to take vacations. Virtually all the executives I worked for at J&J took all their vacation time and they usually did something exotic with it, like fishing in Canada or snorkeling in the Galapagos islands. I learned the ethos of "work hard, play hard." It is a great way to live. Focus on your job and commitments. Deliver. Go take a vacation. But a lot of people I know have trouble taking vacations. They don't. They won't. They can't. Or, they are either guilt-ridden or insecure. Too bad. I know a lot of very successful people with broad responsibilities who know how to enjoy vacations and use them to recharge their physical, mental, emotional, and spiritual batteries.

If I wanted to capture depression in a photograph, for me, it would look like this: blue sky, green water, white beach, and a guy walking in the surf – with a cell phone glued to his ear! If you want to spend 15 minutes a day clearing voicemails and that allows you to relax the rest of the day while on vacation… humph… well, maybe. But really, it is a vacation. Latin for empty. Vacate. Leave. Empty your brain and your psyche and leave the world behind for one to two weeks.

HOW TO PREPARE FOR A VACATION
So, maybe these folks with the cell phone glued to their ear need some help in preparing for a vacation. Maybe you are one of them? If so, read on for help is on the way.

To prepare for a vacation, first anticipate and plan ahead about all the people who will be looking for you and all of the issues that will want to nibble at you while you are away. You will then close things out as much as possible before you go and, most importantly, empower your teammates to make decisions in your absence.

First, you are not omnipotent and you, personally, are not the only one with all the answers. Second, if you can't entrust your team for 5-10 business days, you have not been effective in recruiting your team. Make this the new year resolution. Sanitize your team. Restaff, retool so they are at least competent enough so that you can take a real vacation – next year. Resolve to do it. It will pay huge personal dividends.

HOW TO ACHIEVE A SUCCESSFUL VACATION

You need to anticipate the ankle-biters and speak to them before the vacation. You leave a voicemail and email message to the effect that you are "going on vacation, with limited access to telecommunications. My assistant can be reached at the following extension." And you have reviewed critical issues with him or her ahead of time so they know:

"For sales... call Ed

For marketing... call Gary

For customer service... call Kate

If you need to reach me for an emergency, here is the best number." And I make sure to clearly communicate to my staff that an emergency is truly something major such as – potential loss of a major account, resignation of a key employee, or a death.

I don't get many phone calls. You need these kind of rules if you truly are going to take a vacation. I could give you a very long list of executives and leaders I know who are in terrible physical, mental, emotional, and/or spiritual decay. They are in bad shape. That is not the road I have any interest in following. A brief vacation a couple of times per year is a great way to recharge and stay at peak performance throughout the year and for many years to come. It is also a great way to focus on your family and/or friends and revitalize this important dimension in your life.

Jesus was big on vacations. They were short but they were vacations. He would get away alone to a mountaintop or to a secluded spot on a lake with a handful of his closest disciples. They would all have quality time and recharge themselves.

SOME CONDUCIVE SPOTS

We went on our first cruise recently and it was the best vacation we ever had. It was totally relaxing. There was an incredible feeling of leaving the world behind as we stood on the deck surrounded by ocean on all sides.

There was complete tranquility as I leaned over my veranda rail and stared at the greenish-blue marble-like swirls in the water below. A cool but comfortable breeze bathed my face. A different port of call or beach most days added to the feeling of the "great escape". OK, on day 5, I broke down and checked voicemail. No problems. I didn't check it again until back in port. Next time, I vow to make it seven days without checking any form of messages. I not only thoroughly enjoyed myself but learned how to take a real vacation and I strongly urge you to learn how also.

SAVOR THE WIN. LEARN FROM THE JOURNEY

What did you learn? Again, before you just lurch forward into the next new thing, savor your achievement. Like sports highlight tapes, go over the videotape of your life journey or your recent quest and review your "plays of the day."

Where did you put the principles of grander vision into action? Where were you operating at your core genius? What did you learn about yourself that makes you a more confident and effective visionary?

WHAT WOULD YOU DO AGAIN THAT REALLY WORKED?

I have long kept a log or journal entitled, "Lessons Learned and Easily Forgotten." I am amazed at the things I find written in my log that would make my daily performance so much more effective if I just made some best practices routine. Some personal examples:

- o Run 45 minutes on the treadmill with a thriller movie in the VCR or DVD. It has to be an "action drama can't-wait-to-see-what-happens-next" kind of movie. Time really flies. I am drenched in sweat and the workout is over before I know it.

- o Eat a pink grapefruit half for breakfast. It actually tastes good, has fiber, and is low calorie. It is almost a free meal in the calorie count. I continuously forget about the pink grapefruit.

- And beyond the comparably trivial pursuits like sweat and grapefruits, there are eternal and sublime topics where I easily forget a major life lesson learned such as what I refer to as my "VOG exercise." Get totally silent before the Almighty each morning and just listen to one thought that the voice of God (VOG) places in your heart for the day. I will say more about this shortly.

WHAT DO YOU REGRET AND WILL PREVENT IN THE FUTURE?

I will never react to a situation when I am in a highly negative state. I have learned all too often that if I do, my thinking is clouded, my decisions will be jaded, and I am likely to create a human relations disaster. So, I sleep on it, or put it off to the side and always pray about the matter.

I regret when I cave into the temptation of the 2,000 calorie triple chocolate devil fudge brownie mousse cake for dessert. You know the kind of dessert that restaurants seem to specialize in? I know that I will not sleep well, will hate myself in the morning, set my training program back a week, lower my energy level, and clog my arteries.

I will not make a critical decision until the last moment that it has to be made. I will continue to collect necessary data to make the most informed decision. But once I make the decision, there will be no second-guessing or looking back and I will move on! For more insights on how to develop within you this very important and disciplined approach to decision-making, I suggest two specific books. One I have previously mentioned and that is Stephen Sample's, *The Contrarian's Guide to Leadership*. The other is *In An Uncertain World* by Robert E. Rubin. Mr. Rubin was a senior executive at Goldman Sachs where he spent twenty-six years and then served as U.S. Treasury Secretary from 1995 to 1999.

I will be patient with people and catch myself when self-righteous indignation starts rearing its ugly presence within me. I am about to do or say something that will set back human relations considerably and self-defeat all the hard work that went before it in building up those relations.

These are just some examples of the types of experiences I have had and want to prevent in the future. Truly learn from your regrets and avoid being a recidivist!

PERSONAL ASSESSMENT OF THE JOURNEY
How was the journey? What parts did you like and not like? Did you learn how to – if not enjoy – at least appreciate the journey? Type A humans may be obsessed with the goal or the vision, but God has blessed you with the gift of the day, with the "coincidence," with the accidental tourist or angel who graced your path. There are miracles in your midst each day, once you become sensitized to the presence of the Divine in your life.

TEAM ASSESSMENT OF THE JOURNEY
Replay the highlights film about your team members. These people are only as dedicated and committed and productive as you give them the reason to be. Where did they perform admirably and what was your role? Where did they fall down and were you there to catch them or were you an accomplice in their failure?

RAISE THE BAR. CAST NEW VISIONS
Over the span of my career, I came upon many different approaches to leadership principles and models. I like to think that I eclectically picked up bits and pieces that worked for me across a broad sampling. One of the better models that has become ingrained within my sub-conscience was taught by Rich and Suzie Thomas, two really neat people who were a successful husband-wife team of leadership development and team-building consultants. The model they used focused around five core roles of a leader. These five are:

- o Paint the vision
- o Model the way
- o Encourage the heart
- o Give constructive feedback

- Raise the bar (and cast new visions!)

What I personally like about these five roles are that, for me, they seem logical, linear, and easy to internalize. And, as I have internalized them over the years, depending upon the situation, I find myself asking within such questions like:

"Am I painting the vision? Is it clear?"

"Am I modeling the way? Am I the leader, leading by my example and showing the team how it is done?"

"Beyond task management, am I encouraging the heart of my team-mates?"

"Am I giving constructive coaching and counseling feedback? Or am I just letting people drift as I avoid an obvious conflict that needs addressing?"

"Is it time to raise the bar again– for me, or for my team, or for seeking yet another grander vision?"

See if these five principles around the core roles of a leader can work for you.

INCREMENTS OR TRANSFORMATIONAL

On a daily basis, raise the bar incrementally on what you expect from tasks for yourself and for your expanded team.

On a grander scale, looking at the horizon of a year, 5 years, or 10 years, think transformational in raising the bar. A caterpillar becoming a butterfly – now that's transformational. Think of that as a metaphor for your life. Do you want to be slimy and crawl around in the dirt? Or be beautiful and experience the freedom to fly? Think transformational as your raise the bar on your one and only precious life that God has given you as an ultimate gift. And stay close to God in prayer, immersed in the Owner's Manual, in meditation and in discerning the VOG as you pursue the transformational.

GO BACK TO THE OWNER'S MANUAL

If I need to reset my TV, cell phone, DVD, or similar electronic gadgetry, I must go back to the owner's manual. I labor to figure out the process and sequence.

Hopefully, you will agree that life is more complicated than this modern wizardry and your one and precious life is exponentially more significant. So, when you get to the point where you need to reset your bearings, raise the bar, and hopefully consider transformation, get out the Owner's Manual.

My Owner's Manual is the NIV study Bible. Sometimes, I only have 5 minutes, or another time it might be 2 hours. In either case, it is just an incredible learning and upward alignment experience. I don't make a serious decision without continuously connecting with my Creator through knowledge gained from the Owner's Manual.

SIT DOWN WITH THE OWNER

Remember the concept of energy bursts and making your inner programming line up with your calendar to get the most out of a day? I am an early bird – up at 5:00 a.m., even 4:00 a.m. if I feel rested.

Here is how some of my most valuable life moments are spent: It is early a.m. and still dark out. The crickets are gently chirping. My first cup of coffee is ready. I turn on the gas fireplace.

I sit down with my coffee and, with a heart of gratitude, I connect with God. I proceed through the spiritual terrain of thanksgiving, adoration, contrition, and last, requests. I may read a few psalms or proverbs. Perhaps some of my highlighted passages form the epistles of Paul. Or, I will dwell on the red-letter words of Jesus (special feature of many Bibles).

LISTEN TO THE VOG (VOICE OF GOD) – AND ACT ON IT

Then, I just get quiet– in my mind and in my heart. All anxieties and fears become subdued. I get on my knees and bow my head. I bring myself to an absolute point of reverence, respect, and awe because I am about to approach the awesome Creator of the universe who also made little me in the midst of all this incomprehensible vastness.

Silence. Quiet. Still. I mean totally quiet in the head so nothing will share space here. And then I whisper, "speak to me, Lord, in the quiet of this morning, let me know your will, tell me what to do."

And then a word, a name, or a phrase will be placed in my head or my heart. I am always amazed. The apparent disconnection or variety of what is placed within me, through the VOG, amazes and astonishes. Some examples:

"Focus on the baby." This was strategic direction for my current job challenge.

"Call a certain family member." The time was right for reconciliation.

"Drive safely." My job and other life responsibilities had temporarily overwhelmed me. I was way out of balance and not present in the moment. I was dangerous behind the wheel in this very distracted state.

"Help your pastor." Stop criticizing from the sidelines and get in the game! Roll up your sleeves and get dirty.

"Love your wife totally and unconditionally and view her as a most incredible gift I have given you." Get beyond the really dumb trivialities that mark too many marriages.

"Writer...Write!" (As in a command.) I have long written by hand letters of appreciation or encouragement to people. But somehow, I drifted away from this personal best practice through selfishness or distraction. "Use the gift or lose it," the voice said to me. I started up again.

I could give you so many other examples. I know that there is no good reason that I do not practice the VOG experience each morning. There is no good reason, but I have a bunch of bad reasons. My short list of bad reasons are:

"I don't have time."

"It takes too long."

"I'm not worthy today."

"It's too intense; I'm not awake yet."

"I am afraid that God will tell me something I do not want to hear."

I need to get beyond this. In terms of the leadership concept about "raising the bar," this is the greatest exercise imaginable. One caveat on the subject: if you solicit the voice of God, He will speak. But then you are now expected to ACT on it. God will not grant you this incredible gift if you continuously toss it aside.

Staying close to God through a daily VOG experience is the best way to stay balanced in the area of savoring victories, learning from defeats and continuing onwards and upwards each day in your life and leadership roles. And as you struggle through the normal portion of setbacks that are just part of the journey, remember the words of Don Shula, who is firstly a man of strong faith and second, a world-famous Superbowl winning professional football coach next:

"Failure is not fatal and success is not forever."

Questions For Reflection:
1. Are you a workaholic or can you turn it off and live in the moment of present joy when you are with family or loved ones?

2. Will you allow yourself a break in the action to savor minor and major victories before charging back into full-adrenaline action mode?

3. Do you take time to refresh, renew, reward, and recognize the sacrificial contributions of your team as you achieve key milestones along the way?

4. Do you know how to handle setbacks and defeats? What are the lessons learned? How do setbacks and defeats potentially give you insights for breakthrough thinking?

5. In the midst of victories and defeats, do you stay balanced and remember that at all times– God is in control? Are you ready to practice the VOG exercise? If not, why not? I told you mine. What are your bad excuses? The stakes are huge. Go for it!

Prayer
Dear Lord, through the ups and downs of life and leadership, let me always keep my eyes on the prize which is eternity, a loving father in Heaven, salvation through your Son, and the empowerment of the Holy Spirit. Let me know that your will is being played out because I have surrendered my life (the life that you gave me) back to you unconditionally. I want to live day-by-day the script of the unique life that you planned just for me. Let me accept the outcome. Success is not forever and failure is never fatal in the eternal scheme of things.

Meditation Verse: Psalms 20:4-5
"May he give you the desire of your heart and make all your plans succeed. We will shout for joy when you are victorious and will lift up our banners in the name of our God. May the Lord grant all your requests."

CHAPTER 9

Become God's Leader in the Workplace

But Moses said, "Lord, please send someone else to do it (lead)."
- Exodus 4:13

KNOW WHERE TO PLACE THE GLORY

When I see athletes after a score or great play, thump their chests and point towards Heaven, I think– they know where to place the glory. My question to you is: Do you know where to place the glory for both the daily and lifetime touchdowns of your existence? Get real, truthful, clear – and know where to place the glory.

ALL GLORY AND HONOR IS YOURS

The disciples said to Jesus, "but we don't know how to pray. Please teach us." Jesus replied, "Pray to your Father in Heaven this way" (my paraphrase):
> Our Father who is in Heaven
> Sacred be your name
> Your Kingdom come, your will be done,
> On earth as it is in Heaven.
> Give us this day what we need just for today.
> And forgive us our wrong doings of others,
> As we forgive those who wronged us.
> And give us the grace to
> Avoid temptation and evil.
> For your Grand Vision is the Kingdom
>   The Power
>   And
>   The Glory forever.
>   Amen

FROM SUCCESS TO SIGNIFICANCE

Bob Bufort is the author of two titles, *Half-Time* and *Finishing Well*, which have had a significant impact on my beliefs. In both books, he poses the question, "How do you move your life from success to significance?" It is a fantastic question with eternal implications.

My answer is this: Most of success is measured by all the good things that have happened to you; family, jobs, career, money, house, cars, toys, investments, retirement fund. You get the picture. Mainly, success is all about YOU.

Significance is about the lasting contributions of your life to anyone BUT you. It's about using all of your energy, gifts, and your calling to serve the needs of OTHERS. It is not easy because it is difficult to escape the gravitational pull of SELF but it is possible. I encourage you to read Bob Buford's books regardless of your age. If you are at the "half-time" of your life and you want to finish well, these books are for you. If you are in your twenties and thirties, it is not a bad idea to get a picture of where you are headed through the eyes and voices of many others who have traveled the road ahead of you. Look into both *Half-Time* and *Finishing Well*.

TRUST IN THE LORD OF THE IMPOSSIBLE
But it can be done. You are not in this alone. Lloyd Ogilvie is an accomplished individual of success and significance. He is Pastor Emeritus of First Presbyterian Church, Hollywood, and former Chaplain of the U.S. Senate. Dr. Ogilvie is a communicator, author, and frequent speaker throughout the nation. If I could take only ten books to the proverbial desert island, his work, *Lord of the Impossible*, would be one of them.

I have read and re-read *Lord of the Impossible* several times. One of the more provocative questions he poses is this book is:

"What would you attempt,
if you were sure
that the Lord would intervene to help you?"

What would you do with your life if you had absolutely zero chance of failing and that you knew the Creator of the universe would ensure your success? It is neither a fairytale nor just some academic question. God made the universe timeless and boundaryless; alpha and omega. God made you and me with a purpose, with a unique calling, with a plan.

Listen to the VOG to discern the plan. Read the Owner's Manual to understand the fit between you and your owner. Trust that through the ages, He has been faithful and just to his believers. He will equip you and give you just what you need for the day.

Your faith is required as your part of the bargain. Aligned with this awesome force of the universe, all righteous things are possible. You will find joy, meaning, purpose, significance, and daily movement towards a grander vision.

BECOME GOD'S LEADER IN THE WORKPLACE

Up to now, we have focused on many of the key skills required to be a leader in the workplace regardless if that workplace is for profit, non-profit, or church. We have covered personal preparations, discerning, and focusing on vision, energizing teams, and marshalling resources. We zeroed in on the fundamentals of execution; the ability as a leader to "get it done." Realizing that sometimes we just don't get it done, we addressed dealing with victories and defeats.

Now that we have established a firm foundation of general leadership principles, I want to dial up our focus or as the noted TV chef, Emiril Lagasse would say; "Bam! Let's kick it up a notch!" Let's move from the general realm of being a leader to the specific objective of becoming God's leader in the workplace.

"What does that look like?" you may be asking yourself. Maybe it sounds scary or risky. In the ensuing pages, I hope to dispel these negative thoughts and inform you of what it looks like, how it will actually help your enterprise, and will energize you to jump out of bed in the morning with an incredible sense of purpose.

Based on observations, extensive reading, discussions with other men and women of faith, and most importantly, my own trials and errors over many years, I have developed a point-of-view on the "Best Practices" of people who step out in their faith and live as God's leader in the workplace.

BEST PRACTICES OF GOD'S WORKPLACE LEADERS

Most Christians go to work each day searching for that Godly connection they had on Sunday, yet wondering how it dissipated by lunchtime on Monday. From personal experience, I know it does not need to be this way.

I have wrestled with this issue for most of my thirty years in the working world. I continuously asked and struggled with the answer to the question, "What does it take to be God's leader in the workplace?" Beyond my leadership experience in the business realm, I am also drawing on experiences from my leadership positions in the military, local politics, government, and from my church. I believe the best practices are relevant and applicable whether your environment is in the profit or non-profit world.

I have attempted to capture all of these experiences and interactive observations into The Five Best Practices of God's Workplace Leaders. With an understanding of these best practices, you can be well on your way to becoming God's leader in the workplace.

Best Practice #1:

Seeing God's Hand in every aspect of your life including your work.

God made everything! He made you and me, our universe and the sustenance on the planet that we seek and produce via our work. It is critical to understand that our work is important to God and God expects us to work. Work is not some kind of "downtime" in your spiritual life and journey. As a matter of Biblical fact, God commands us to work both before the fall (Genesis 2:15) and after the fall (Genesis 3:17-19). Beyond these dimensions, Rick Warren, in his massive best-seller *The Purpose Driven Life*, imparted to me the concept that we will also have a special job to work when we get to heaven! So, work is not some anti-spiritual entity. Work is a key part of our being, who we are, what we do, and our very existence.

God's workplace leaders understand that there are not compartments of God's time and work time but that all time belongs to God, including those hours we spend at work. So, by starting with this understanding, the committed Christian goes forth into the work world with the mindset of, "What does God expect of my attitudes and behaviors on the job? How can I live a reflection of my faith? How can I serve others with all the gifts and talents with which I have been uniquely blessed?"

Best Practice 2:

Praying continuously, earnestly and specifically for God to unveil to you that special vision of your faith at work.

It can be a tough road becoming God's leader in the workplace, particularly if you think you can do it by yourself. You can only do it in partnership with God and the way to cement that partnership is through prayer. Pray specifically in asking God what does he want you to do with your time and talent in the workplace.

At one point in my career, I wrestled with entering seminary but it just did not feel right. The conflict was "how do I fully serve the Lord if it is not as a full-time, black-robed ordained minister?" My senior pastor of our church advised me that God needed people like me out in the workplace 24/7 to be salt and light. This could be part of my calling. Additionally, I had achieved what the world would consider "success" as president of a business division of a large global healthcare company. My pastor said this gave me a currency of credibility out in the world that he could never achieve from the pulpit. If a minister proclaims the gospel of Christ from the pulpit, the normal reaction of people is – "we expect that; he is a minister." But if someone with a position of secular achievement and success proclaims the gospel of Christ, the reaction of people is often – "what's going on here?"

This conversation with my pastor took place about 10 years ago and, as a result, I embarked on a focused regimen of prayer asking God for clarity around his vision of my mission as one of his leaders in the workplace.

Best Practice 3:

Trusting God to equip and deliver you to that vision for which you are called.

If God has called you, he will equip you and he will deliver you. These are critical points so let me be clear on the meaning and implication of each of these words. It took me a long time to understand them.

- God **calls** you. By calling, I mean a specific Divine appointment where you are in submission to God's will and you are living God's plan for your life. The Bible says, "Many are called but few are chosen." I have long interpreted this phrase to mean that God calls many people but few choose to accept the call. Most people live very hectic, distracted, and noisy lives. There is so much noise that they cannot hear the whisper of God's call.

- God **equips** you. If you answer God's call and prayerfully walk with him, he will equip you. Equip means God will provide you with the skills, plans, inspiration, and insights needed to achieve your mission. He equipped Moses to take on pharaoh and he will equip you to take on the workplace. He will place in your mind the words you need to say when you need to say them. He will provide the grace of the moment to deal with difficult people or difficult situations.

- God will **deliver** you. Despite equipping you, the challenges will be continuous and, at times, significant. But you must have faith, persistence, and resilience that through it all God will ultimately deliver you. Deliver means that there will be challenges, frustrations, and setbacks which may cause you to tire or have doubt. But persist in strength with your faith for God will deliver you to his finish line.

Best Practice #4:
Stepping out in faith not fear in all work situations.

God's workplace leaders are self-aware of what is going on with them spiritually through all the task stresses and interpersonal challenges that occur throughout the day. Once you consciously decide that you will live out your faith at work, you must overcome all of the wily ploys of the Evil One. If this is new term, let me explain that the Evil One is Satan; the Devil; the Fallen

Angel; the Negative Force in our universe. I will not go into the theology of it here. The majority of Americans believe in the existence of the Devil so I will leave it at that. But the bulk of the mainstream media and secular sources of power in society send a very different message. To wit, they want you to believe that "there is no Devil...you just had a bad day." Theologically and biblically, it is 100% clear that there is a devilish evil force in the universe attempting to influence us into wrong choices and lifestyles 24/7. I will also point out that most people and enterprises that do the Devil's work spend a great amount of time trying to convince the public that the Evil One does not exist in the first place. But I am writing from a majority view that evil and the Evil One exist. And I believe that he continuously attempts to thwart our efforts to live life as God intended it.

My good friend and mentor, Dr. Stephen Payne, who is the president of his firm, Leadership Strategies, Inc., has coined a great line which sounds all the more impactful with his elegant British accent. The line is this,

"All chit-chat comes from the Evil One."

Chit-chat is the derived term to mean all the self-doubt, negative, angry, apprehensive, anxious, fearful thoughts and voices that can swirl in your head at times. Sometimes it is a well-placed dagger in your heart or mind. The chit-chat takes on many stripes and includes the planting of uncertainty, doubt, fear, rationalization, and appeals to ego. It is all intended to sink you, sabotage you, and throw you off the path of becoming God's leader in the workplace. All these ploys; this "chit-chat," are the work of the Evil One.

The everyday gravitational-like pulls of this world are around the cluster of sex, money, power, politics, position and perks, status, fame, and fortune. (Does that about cover it?) But if you are stepping out in faith, your entire mind, body, heart, and soul should be centered around the cluster of: God, eternity, the kingdom, life on earth as temporary assignment, and work as part of your created purpose. You should also recognize that leadership is a gift and is expected to be a Divine partnership.

The Bible is full of stories of leaders who were called by God and their initial responses were significantly less than heroic. Moses was retired and tending sheep in a comfortable pasture when God called him into action. Moses' response can be paraphrased as:

"You talking to me, God?"

"You can't mean me, God?"

"I can't do it, God."

"I am not a leader."

"I am not capable."

"I am not a good speaker."

"Can't someone else do it?"

If you find yourself responding in a similar fashion as Moses, take heart and pray! Pray that God gives you the grace that you would fully surrender and, in doing so, end up as his incredible courageous leader in the workplace and a heroic leader like Moses became. Read the story of Moses in Exodus; the second book of the Bible, to see how Moses became one of the greatest of God's leaders in the workplace of all time. And then live the best practice of stepping out in faith, not fear!

Best Practice #5:

Living a credo of *People First. Results Always!*

It is critical to understand that delivering results and being one of God's leaders in the workplace are not mutually exclusive. One of the most effective leaders that ever worked for me was Al Altomari, or Alto as he is more commonly known. Alto was not the kind of person to wear his faith on his sleeve but everything about this guy's life proclaimed that he was a man of integrity and I knew him to be a man committed to his Creator and his faith. The way he acted on the job, with his wife, his kids, in his community, on non-profit boards, or caring for his infirmed parents, all combined a drive for achievement and a passion for people.

Alto and I spent many years working together and many hours discussing life and work. As his boss, I think I taught him a lot but he is such a talented individual on so many fronts that I learned a lot from him as well. He always delivered results and his people loved him. Quite a tough act to pull off, as you may know. I would periodically ask him, "How do you do it?" His consistent response was:

"People First. Results Always!"

His people knew that he cared for them. He cared that they learned their skills so they could be effective, be personally satisfied, and deliver results. He cared that they perform at the high end of their abilities, feel like contributors, and earn the high end of their compensation. He cared about their development and preparing them for future positions of increased responsibility. He cared about the trials and travails of their personal situations– married, divorced, single, engaged, separated. Alto would listen and offer wisdom and support within boundaries while they worked through their issues.

Through it all, he expected his team to do their jobs and deliver results– like he did. He led by example; the first rule of leadership. And, in doing so, he drove the credo of–
"People First. Results Always!"

In Summary:

Synthesizing the Best Practices of God's Workplace Leaders

God desires that his relationship with us to be 24/7. The time we spend in the workplace is a huge block and God calls us to live out our faith at work. There are very many ways that you can live out your faith at work. In addition to the profile of Alto captured above, there are many situations that may either be a trial or an opportunity for your faith. Some examples:

- Talk casually with a colleague about a work insight you received from someone at your church or from your minister. Let people know that your faith is a key part of who you are.

- When people come to you with significant problems, listen, show empathy, and tell them you will pray for them. (Then make sure you do!)

- When people have babies, write them a short note or send a card of joy and let your faith shine through.

- When people experience a death in their family, write a personal note of sympathy that comes from your heart and is a reflection of your faith.

I have consciously attempted to do all the above for over 15 years now and I have never had a negative reaction from anyone. To the contrary, half the time I hear a "thank you" and half the time I get a "you don't know how much that meant to me."

In addition to these specific examples, there are many general behaviors that are a witness for God as you act out your faith at work. Consider the following:

- Work to a higher standard than what your boss expects of you; work to the standards that God has set for you. Are you giving your job the 100% that is your obligation for the compensation that you agreed to? Do you cut corners when your boss or peers are not aware? Work to a higher standard for God is looking and expecting your best 100%.

- What about that expense account? The higher you go in an organization, the more are the discretionary spends that are accessible to you. Many judgments are shades of gray. But God's leaders err on the side of God's higher standards; not those of the accounting department.

- What about all the ego games at work? How are you holding up in this area? In the grand scheme of things, does it really matter whose office is two feet larger or who got invited to a special meeting that you didn't?

- How are you doing at office politics? Political realities from higher up in an organization often shape an outcome and to be an effective leader you must be on top of the situation. But are you engaging in petty politics? Are you using your position for unfair political advantage with peers or subordinates? Be aware and catch yourself.

- What about language? At one time, I spoke two languages– one with my church crowd and one with my office crowd. It dawned on me one day that I would be mortified if my pastor heard me at work. It then occurred to me that I ought to be mortified because, one, God knew, and two, most people knew I was a committed Christian. What in the world kind of perverse message was I communicating about who I was and what my faith was all about? It takes discipline to overcome the stresses, frustrations, and breakdowns that occur in most any organization. But it can be done if you ask for God's help. Control your tongue and be a living witness for Him.

- Last, how is your head game? How is your heart game? Do you just make it through the day fraught with fears, doubts, and chronic performance anxiety? Or, do you go through the day with faith, hope, love, confidence, and security knowing that God walks with you? If you are praying to the One and Only Almighty God of the universe, then the latter is how it should be.

God is faithful to his followers. God supports his followers who answer the call. He equips and he delivers. He will never forget us nor forsake us. He will be with us always even until the end of time.

You do not have to be a frazzled mess of stress by lunchtime on Monday. In prayerful partnership with the eternal Lord and creator, you can become God's leader in the workplace.

Questions For Reflection:
1. In the midst of accomplishments and life achievements, do I keep a humble heart and know where to place the glory?

2. Whether or not I have had achievements or aspire for even greater earthly success, am I on a track towards significance?

Success is all about me. Significance is measured by the lasting positive impact I am having on others. How am I doing? Are any mid-course corrections required?

3. Am I ready to become one of God's leaders in the workplace? Why not? What is holding me back? Is it fear, embarrassment, laziness, lack of focus or lack of prayer? Other?

4. If I truly believed that I had zero chance of failure when I commit myself to Godly plans empowered by the Holy Spirit, would I now take the plunge and become God's leader in the workplace?

5. How do I measure up versus the best practices of God's workplace leaders? What practices can I start doing tomorrow? Where do I need some prayerful help and guidance?

Prayer

Dear Lord, thank you for all of the gifts and talents that you have bestowed upon me. Let me never forget that leadership is one of those gifts. I pray that I be found worthy to measure up to your call of leadership in the workplace. Let me lead humbly yet fearlessly, knowing that I am empowered by the Holy Spirit. Thank you, Lord. Amen.

Meditation Verse: Psalm 4:3
"Know that the Lord has set apart the godly for himself; the Lord will hear when I call him."

CHAPTER 10

Onwards and Upwards: Casting Grander Visions

"Come, follow me, and I will make you fishers of men."
- Matthew 4:19

The focus of the preceding chapter was becoming God's leader in the workplace and the best practices that propel these leaders. In this final chapter, we want to move onwards and upwards and take a quantum leap on what a grander vision of your leadership can be all about. To facilitate this effort, I want to share with you the inspiring profiles of a dozen of God's leaders who have stepped out in faith and taken the step to expanded ministry leadership beyond their starts in the workplace.

Once again, the words of Bill Hybels saying, "Enough...enough," echo in my ears. Bill's challenge at a leadership summit was, "when is enough...enough?" What does it take to say, "I have enough." What does it take to reach the point where you say, "I have enough money, enough security, enough admiration of my community, enough ego gratification, enough trophies..." I think you get the picture...enough!

The challenge is to think beyond success in the business world and find ways to apply your enormous God-given talents to transform the world at large. Do not misunderstand me. I applaud and uphold the professionals and leaders slogging away every day in the business world. I hold it on a pedestal. From my experiences has evolved a thinking pattern that goes like this:

All good economic things in this world originate in the profit-making business enterprise. I think profits are good. I think extreme profits are very good (assuming you have complied with all laws regarding fair competition). You cannot generate extreme profits however you want to define them unless you are producing a social good that is highly valued by lots of people and few competitors have figured out how to do it better.

Then we look at the world of non-profits, religious, academic, and government entities. All of these institutions have some level of cash flow– but where did the cash come from? In 9 out of 10 instances, the cash came from profit-making companies or foundations. And what are foundations? Well, if you take a look at the 10 largest foundations, you will see that they are sprinkled with names like Ford, Rockefeller, Carnegie, Mellon, Hewlitt, Packard. So, foundations are huge perpetual savings accounts started with funds that came out of profit-making businesses. I conclude again that profits are a good thing and the source of virtually all wealth creation in a free society.

Then why am I suggesting that you say "enough" and apply your skills in other areas besides business? If you want to stay in business, I am not passing a judgment that that is bad. But I am suggesting that, with the financial freedom you have likely accumulated, you may have enough money to do something where personal money accumulation is not the first priority.

Also, no institutions teach the much-valued and learned skills such as leadership, administration, personal development, finances, and fund-raising like business does. So, if you have accumulated these skills and talents, think of how transformational you could be if you applied them to the local church, local government, a Habitat for Humanity, a Campus Crusade for Christ, World Vision, or thousands of other similar opportunities. I am suggesting that you could move beyond being a profit-making machine (which is a good thing) and transform yourself into a Spirit-propelled Kingdom-making machine (which is an awesome thing!). I am talking about expanding the kingdom of Heaven here on earth.

Maybe this sounds like too much of a stretch or too far-fetched for you. So, let me introduce you to some people who have made this jump from the business world to the Spirit world. Meet some people whose lives and leadership reflect a grander vision and who are transforming our world.

THE CHURCH AT LIBERTY CORNER –
STEVE MCCONNELL

The Presbyterian Church at Liberty Corner (also known as Liberty Corner Presbyterian Church, or LCPC most commonly) was a cozy little church nestled in the sleepy hamlet of Liberty Corner, a historical site, for close to 125 years. The membership was about 300 for as long as anyone could remember until Steve McConnell appeared on the scene in 1990.

Great things have happened at Liberty Corner over the last 15 years under Steve's leadership with lots of people casting grander visions. Official membership is now about 1000 with the community served estimated at 2000. Significant expansions of ground and facilities enable LCPC to offer:

The Children's Corner is a daycare center, which plays a vital role in the community and provides a wonderful opportunity to reach the hitherto unreached for The Lord.

Center Court is a huge family life center which seats 500 and is home to a popular contemporary service on Sunday mornings. The space can be reset for basketball or reset to feed the masses which it does on a regular basis. It is also being opened up to the community on an increasing basis providing another great outreach program.

The Appalachian Service Project, or ASP, is an annual event where recently close to 100 people gave up their personal or vacation time to go to Appalachia to work on homes with the mission of making them warmer, drier, and safer. And, in the process, they strike up human relationships that transcend socioeconomic situations.

Hearts For Honduras is a mission outreach program that started as a spark and now is a blazing bonfire of the Lord. Lay leaders took charge of this project and decided to team-up and adopt a sister church in La Entrada, Honduras. The goals were to provide some basic housing, medical and dental services, and, most importantly, to set up a school. The school is established and taken root and is such a breakthrough in this repressed and depressed area. The school offers education, Spiritual development, and hope for a future. The vision continues to grow and, over the years, the program has continued to add more grades.

These are just a smattering of the growth that has taken place at LCPC under the leadership of Steve McConnell and the hundreds of lay leaders he has recruited who decided to step out and move onwards and upwards in pursuit of a grander vision.

My experience at LCPC over 15 years has enabled me to see upfront and personal numerous examples where God's leaders in the workplace can either make significant contributions in pursuit of grander visions either as retirees or while still in the workplace. Below are several examples where individual leaders have pursued a grander vision while still in the job and in their everyday workplace of building the kingdom of God on earth and transforming our world right now through the institution of our local church.

HEARTS FOR HONDURAS – DOUG LIGUORI

I mentioned the Hearts For Honduras program as one of the most successful at Liberty Corner and one of the key leaders is a former pharmaceutical director that said, "enough." As he turned 56, Doug Liguori figured he had enough money to live a comfortable yet simple life on his savings and retirement money. As a global information systems director, Doug was no stranger to international travel. But it was usually business class travel to business class hotels funded by the company expense account. It was a trip to a remote location in Honduras called "La Entrada" that opened up Doug's heart, mind, and soul to a different world. Our church partnership with a sister church in La Entrada was an early vision just taking form. Doug answered the call to take a major leadership position with this venture. Each year, more and more church members volunteered for the annual mission trip to La Entrada. The scope of the services expanded. There is an eye clinic as well as a dental clinic. There was a classroom, now there is a school, grades Kindergarten through 6. The first graduation was held in November 2004 and nearly all of the students continued to seventh grade. This was a wonderful achievement as over half the children in Honduras do not go past fourth grade. Scholarships are provided for the children to continue their education. (Now there are plans to finish up grades 7 and 8. Big thinking is forming around a high school.) Computers have been donated. In the midst of all of this, the gospel is shared in thought, word, and deed. Doug goes down to La Entrada several times a year prior to the annual mission trip to follow up and prepare. And when he isn't working on Honduras, he is somewhere in our church, as head of the Trustees, looking for a leaky roof or a room that needs remodeling or a way to get more parking spaces. In short, Doug is living a grander vision and loving every moment of it.

WILLIE'S TAVERNE BIBLE STUDY – JACK WELCH

Jack Welch is a local entrepreneur who feeds the masses. He does this through the various restaurants he and his partners own in central New Jersey. One of his many restaurants, which happens to be my favorite, is Willy's Taverne in Bedminster, New Jersey. Jack also owns The Store, as well as very family-friendly restaurants named The Famished Frog and The Thirsty Turtle. Jack has started over twenty restaurants since he and his roommate at Cornell graduated with a dream of a career in the restaurant business. Jack also has branched into feeding the masses with his venture, Growth Catering. There are many community events at our local church where Jack's trucks, tents, and people are in full force. Jack loves the parable about Jesus feeding the five thousand because he says the most he has ever fed is 500 and that nearly broke the operation from all the stress and pressure involved. But I think Jack's biggest contribution to kingdom building is something he has been doing close to twenty years now. He makes his restaurants available for Bible studies 6:30 in the morning. I attended these for many years and greatly benefited from them. Hot coffee, fresh Danish, the fellowship of men, and 60 minutes in the Word every Friday morning to cap off the week and start the weekend. Jack has touched thousands of individuals in this way and brought them closer to a knowledge, understanding, and relationship with God the Father, Son and Holy Spirit.

THE AMERICAN DREAM – BARRY ABELL

One of the individuals that I met though the Friday morning Bible studies at Willies Taverne is Barry Abell. Here is his story.

Every workday, Barry Abell was up at 5 a.m. and out the door of his New Jersey home by 6:00 a.m. He drove to the train station, then rode a commuter train across the Hudson River to lower Manhattan; center to the financial world. He walked to a prestigious firm on Wall Street, where he was a municipal bond trader.

At his desk by 7:30, he read at least three newspapers by 8:00 a.m., when the bond market opened. For the next 9 hours, his world was a frenzy of noise and activity– telephones ringing, traders juggling two conversations at a time, constant pressure, millions of dollars riding on a single phone call.

He loved it and he made a lot of money.

At night, he would head home to his two-story colonial home on a two-acre lot in Mendham, New Jersey. He had a beautiful wife, two children, two cars, a swimming pool in the backyard, a dog, a cat, tropical fish, and luxurious vacations.

He was 35 years old.
He was on top of the world.
He was living the American dream.

Then, Barry and his wife, Pam, became followers of Jesus Christ. Their priorities began to change. Barry saw a divorce rate on Wall Street of nearly 75% and felt a deep need to help. Soon a ministry was established called The New York Fellowship, which worked to meet the emotional and spiritual needs of Wall Street executives as well as those of homeless and orphans. Soon the enjoyment and fulfillment of helping others became greater than the earning potential on Wall Street. Barry and Pam made a decision to give up that earthly security for serving in a full-time ministry. Today, they present marriage conferences around the world and continue to work with business executives and their spouses. Their only regret is that they did not make that decision sooner.

GOD'S LAWYER – ELLEN O'CONNELL, ESQ.

Ellen O'Connell is a bundle of energy and intelligence wrapped up in Irish wit and humor. Ellen has been an attorney for over 30 years and spent much of her career in large corporate law practices. She then tried a small partnership for awhile and in recent years took the plunge and hung out her own shingle– right across the street from our church. This is only fitting since I call Ellen 'God's attorney-at-law.' In addition to practicing law, Ellen has held many administrative positions within the New Jersey State Bar Association, and was Chairman of the board of a legal services project that provides free legal services to the disabled.

These positions have given Ellen a powerful place at the table of policy making where she has been highly effective at pushing back the culture and keeping God, Faith, Christian values, the Ten Commandments, the rights of the disabled, and similar matters still supported by New Jersey law. She has done this with the talents God has given her which I alluded to above– energy, intelligence, Irish wit and humor. Throughout the years, Ellen did all this while employed by someone else. And with that came the constraints of struggling with "political correctness" and the subtle pressures of your employer who might not agree with your positions. Now that Ellen is out on her own, the spirits of the Dark Force on this planet must shudder at the possibilities that this talented woman can now accomplish as God's attorney-at-law.

THE PRICELESS EXECUTIVE – ANDY STEWART

I know this is forming a pattern here, but I cannot help it. It was the stratosphere of great people I was blessed to orbit in my J&J world. Andy Stewart was a twenty-five year man at Johnson and Johnson and when I first met him towards the end of his career there, he was Vice-President of Sales at the Ethicon Business Unit. Andy spent his whole career in and around hospitals talking to doctors and nurses and other healthcare professionals about surgery and sutures. He said "enough" when he took an early retirement package at age 55. After golfing his brains out for about six months, he accepted a position as Chairman of the Board of a local hospital for a salary of zero. We spent time together as elders at our local NJ church. Andy brought a lot of passion as well as an attempt to incorporate some business' best practices to help our church with operational excellence as we struggled with the transition from small church to big church. We wanted our pastor to spend most of his time doing what he does best– be our spiritual leader– and we recommended hiring a full-time Director of Operations to run the day-to-day operations of the church which is a full-time focus. We wanted somebody who was probably making $200,000 in the business world and we were willing to pay $80,000 to this person. All the wrong people applied and then the rest of the elders and the Finance committee decided that we just did not have the funds to afford it. This was a disappointing outcome but I guess God had a grander idea. Andy decided he would stop working for the hospital for zero and he would start working for the church for zero. Well, zero plus the flexibility to take off and play golf once or twice a week as the urge dictated. We all thought that was a tremendous bargain for the church and a year later, Andy is having a blast; our Senior Pastor, Steve McConnell, is harnessing his energy where he does things best and we have incorporated just enough business best practices to balance God's need for excellence but also accepting people as they are where they are.

CORPORATE CONTROLLER BY DAY; SENIOR PASTOR BY NIGHT– CLARENCE LOCKETT

I need to share with you a profile of one of the most inspiring role models I had the honor of knowing and like many others, he, too was a career employee and senior executive at Johnson and Johnson. When I met Clarence Lockett towards the end of his pharmaceutical career, he was the Corporate Controller (Chief Accounting Officer) of J&J. Any executive position at a large corporation like J&J is demanding in terms of hours but also mental preoccupation almost 24/7. On top of this, as a corporate officer, Clarence had many additional responsibilities. But here is what made him one of my role models: on top of all of this, he was the Senior Pastor of a growing evangelical church in Pennsylvania. He preached most Sundays and assumed much of the administrative responsibilities as well. When I asked him how he possibly could do this; how could he possibly find the time, he told me, "I just do it. I just do it. God makes it all work out somehow."

Clarence was also well known for his Tuesday lunch time Bible study that he led in one of the conference rooms at corporate headquarters. I asked him, "Did you have to get permission to teach a Bible study?" He responded, "No, I didn't ask anyone." I asked him, "Aren't there legal controversies about corporate Bible studies?" He responded, "I don't know. Nobody has said anything to me about legal concerns. It is the gospel of Jesus Christ. How can there be any concerns about that? Why would you have any concerns about that?" Ouch! I was at the same time ashamed and inspired. I think of Clarence often but always when I see the verse from Paul in the book of Romans (1:16): "For I am not ashamed of the gospel of Jesus Christ; it is the power of God for salvation to everyone who has faith."

Clarence retired from J&J at the age of 55 and, as you might have guessed, he is putting all of his time, talent and energy into his calling as Senior Pastor of his church.

THE LITTLE FEET – TOM FERGUSON

I first met Tom Ferguson in the early 1990's when I worked at Johnson and Johnson Corporate. Tom was the founder of Thomas Ferguson Advertising and was the agency used by many of the Johnson and Johnson companies. What brought him to my attention was not so much his advertising but rather all these people I heard talking about "Tom Ferguson". Things like…"what a great guy"…"what a fun guy to be with"…"what charisma this guy has." So, I just picked up the phone one day, even though I had no need for advertising, and called him and said something to the effect, "I have heard so much about you, I would like to meet you." He jumped at the opportunity to meet a potential future client– which did materialize years later– but a great relationship was birthed immediately. Tom was as charismatic and inspiring as everyone said he was. He was and is one of the most constantly energized, God-fearing, faith-based Big Thinkers I have ever met. He is a friend, colleague in faith, and an important role model and mentor for me.

Tom's grander vision included selling his agency for more money than most of us will only dream about and then turning his energies to the endeavors of non-profit, charitable, church related, political, health-related, and Christian organizations. It seemed like every few months, Tom was launching another Big Idea. He became very vocal and visible in support of the unborn and a staunch voice of the Pro-Life movement. This cost him a lot of former "friends" and business associates. But he charges forward. He always wears the emblem of the little baby feet of the unborn on his spiffy blazer. He puts his name to and raises funds for a drug rehabilitation unit, for several Christian schools, for the Epilepsy foundation, for a new wing of a local hospital, for a new addition to his local church, for the political re-election of his son, Michael, who is our local U.S. Representative, and an "apple who did not fall far from the tree."

Tom has taught me so much about how to conduct one's self whether in the boardroom or the golf course. He generously invites friends to play with him at some very nice golf clubs. He has taught me how to host outings, repair ball marks, tell jokes, and treat everyone like a valuable human being. Everybody from the front desk, to the caddies, to the Pro Shop loves Tom and they will tell you that unsolicited. The fact that he is a big tipper doesn't hurt but it is the total Tom they love. "Don't be so cheap. Throw some money around to these people," Tom first exhorted me. "They are living on minimum wage and you are this big shot J&J executive. Come on!" I have never forgotten that lesson. Or this one: "what do you mean you don't contribute to your college?" After all that experience did to launch your career? And it is so critical to a college's ability to raise money on what percentage of alumni contribute. So, "Come on, contribute."

Tom's life, leadership, and outlook are one continuous grander vision and he constantly prods others to think in these terms too.

GOODBYE ALCOA; HELLO UNION – CHARLES WHITAKER

Charles Whitaker is my father-in-law so I have a fairly accurate and up-close perspective on his grander vision. First of all, I need to say that he is one of the most decent, caring, and Godly men I have ever met. So, whatever he decided to do years ago would likely be blessed and propelled by God's Holy Spirit. Charles is a mechanical engineer by education via Clemson and then he launched on a long corporate career with Alcoa Corporation in the engineering department. He experienced a couple of decades of the promotions, relocations, and reorganizations when one day, he said, "Enough. Sandra (my mother-in-law), let's move back to Union." And that is what they did. They moved back to the small town of Union, South Carolina where they both grew up, dated, and eventually married. After Alcoa, Charles launched the pursuit of a new career as a self-employed entrepreneur. He dabbled as a manufacturer's representative but found his calling as the town surveyor. He traded in his pinstriped suit for a set of overalls, a panama hat, and trekking through underbrush in 95 degree weather most days looking for surveying markers. But the grander vision was that he became a lot more than just the town surveyor. Our family would joke that he became the employer of last resort in Union. He will hire the down and out, the unemployable, and those with previous criminal records. He will give them another chance to amend for their botched life (like Christ did for us). He will literally bail them out. He will try to impart some basic common sense advice to them. But first and last, he leads by example as salt and light and is a constant witness to his faith and his God either in word or in deed. With his career transition to town surveyor, Charles has touched and changed the lives and hearts of so many over the years. His life and his work is a reflection of a grander vision.

FROM SYRACUSE TO BURNSVILLE – RICK DEAN

Rick Dean is about six foot six, I would imagine, and not a pound under 250 to be conservative. Add in the shaved head and you have a potentially intimidating persona. But Rick is one of the gentlest yet strongest, most caring yet toughest people I have ever met. And he is the Senior Pastor of our adopted summertime church in Burnsville, North Carolina, at the local Methodist church. Rick is a big man with an even bigger vision for himself, his congregation, and the world at large. Rick definitely qualifies as one of God's leaders with a grander vision. But he was not always the Senior Pastor at the local church. Rick played college basketball at Syracuse University where he was an All-American and was drafted to play in the NBA. But instead of that draft, right after college, he volunteered to serve in the Army. After Officers basic training, Airborne and Ranger schools, he served as a second lieutenant, Infantry Platoon Leader in Vietnam, with the 101st Airborne Division. He has many stories and lessons learned about God, life, death, leadership, and human beings from that experience. After the army, he went into the FBI followed by a twenty-year career as a teacher and school administrator. At around age 48, he answered the call of God to go into full-time ministry as a pastor. He told me that he really did not want to do this because of a lot of practical uncertainties, but that he knew two things for certain. One, it was the voice of God directing him; and second, you must always be obedient to the word of God. Rick is very inspiring as a pastor, as a role model for a disciple, and in building the kingdom on earth. There is no question in my mind that Rick is a man of grander visions.

FROM SILICON VALLEY TO LITITZ, PA – MIKE BRICKLEY

Mike Brickley is the president of The Pocket Testament League. The mission of the league is to mobilize and equip Christians to "read, carry, and share the word of God." The league was started in 1893 by Helen Cadbury, who shared pocket-sized versions of the Gospel with her friends. Members of the league commit to read the Bible daily, carry the Bible or a tract with them wherever they go, and share it when opportunities arise. Over 8,000,000 people have become members of The Pocket Testament League.

Mike had a very successful career in business before he moved to The Pocket Testament. He has a BA from Bates College, an MBA from Rutgers University, and is a CPA. As a Christian businessman, Mike was recognized for building a financial services company that was included in the INC 500 as the 34th fastest growing private company in America. He was also Chairman of the Board of Directors of Silicon Valley Bank; a bank that serves emerging technology companies and has grown to over four billion dollars in assets.

At The Pocket Testament, Mike has transferred his leadership and financial skills from business-building to building the kingdom of God on earth.

WILLOW CREEK (The Rest of the Story) – BILL HYBELS

Bill Hybels said, "Enough" when he was twenty years old. His father was a very successful entrepreneur who ran a prosperous produce business. It was expected that Bill would step into the family business. But there was a small inner voice that called him with a different idea, direction, and purpose. The big idea planted within him, which still rankles many mainstream church pastors I am sure, goes something like the following: "If God is so good, why are so many churches and religious experiences so bad?" It seemed that "doing church," as we commonly know it, was just a turnoff to masses of people (no play on words intended). Bill was called to pursue starting a church that would be biblically based, Christ-centered, and what today is called "conservative evangelical" but would have none of the trappings or turnoffs of traditional churches. There would be no robes, stain-glass windows, statues, or pews. There would be a lot of singing and music, sermons based on the Bible, Bible studies and small groups that would meet outside of church on Sunday to study the Bible. (Have you seen the word Bible a lot in this paragraph?) Bill and a handful of friends started this new church in an old movie theatre that was in need of a tenant. The story is an entrepreneurial adventure of its own in terms of how to fund a major venture when you do not have funds. But they did it. Today, twenty-five plus years later, this little venture is now Willow Creek Community Church in Barrington, Illinois outside Chicago. The campus is hundreds of acres and various buildings that house worship centers, learning centers, and an array of ministries. Willow serves over 18,000 attendees on a typical weekend. There are many elements of success that went into this happening, but one in particular that I would like to impress upon you is the role and the power of lay leadership in driving this success. One of the critical success factors underlying the success of Willow (beyond its core value of staying true to the Bible) was enrolling hundreds of people with "worldly success" into leadership positions. These were both full-time paid staff positions and volunteers. Individuals with Harvard MBAs and Fortune 500 corporate experience; entrepreneurs, physicians, lawyers, Broadway musicians and vocalists have all thrown in their lot with this big idea that came from the small voice over twenty-five years ago. Willow Creek will always be etched in my mind as an example of "a grander vision" that came to fruition. It took time, talent, prayer, and leadership. But it was a huge vision that became a reality.

Questions For Reflection:

1. Have you had "enough?" If not, what do you envision will be enough personal achievement for you as measured through the eyes of the world and your fellow man?

2. Is there a "significance" ministry that you can launch right now on a part-time or transitional basis?

3. With what you now know, do you have a grander vision of leadership for your life and your chosen roles? What are the dimensions of it?

4. How intense is and should your prayer life be as you seek God's guidance on this most important assignment?

5. When you pray, are you praying to a small God (in your own mind) or a grander vision God who can move heaven and earth to achieve his designed outcomes?

Prayer

Heavenly Father, thank you for the gift and the favor of blessing me with the skills of leadership. I am your committed leader so now, Lord, I pray that you might launch me onwards and upwards towards the grander vision you have designed for me. Empower me with your Holy Spirit. I pray this in your Son's name. Amen.

Meditation Verse: Matthew 25:21
"His master replied, 'Well done, good and faithful servant! You have been faithful with a few things; I will put you in charge of many things. Come and share your master's happiness.'"

CONCLUDING COMMENTS

I hope that in the course of these pages I have given you a stimulus to look at your life and your leadership potential, no matter what your endeavor in much bigger terms. I pray that you will now pursue a grander vision for it all. To wrap it all up, the salient beliefs that I have attempted to convey which can be transformational for you, God's kingdom and this world are:

- You do not walk alone in leadership
- You have been given a special gift and are expected to use that gift
- You are in a great partnership with the God of Creation. He is the senior partner and you are the junior partner
- You can become God's leader in your workplace and maybe even one day move Onwards and Upwards to full-time ministry in support of an even grander vision!

SUGGESTED READING FOR DEVELOPING A GRANDER VISION:

The Bible (New International Version) – Zondervan Publishers

Lord of The Impossible – Lloyd Ogilvie

My Utmost For His Highest - Oswald Chambers

The Purpose Driven Life – Rick Warren

Courageous Leadership – Bill Hybels

Halftime – Bob Buford

Finishing Well – Bob Buford

Visioneering – Andy Stanley

The Effective Executive – Peter Drucker

The 7 Habits of Highly Effective People – Stephen Covey

The Contrarian's Guide to Leadership – Stephen Sample

Everyone's A Coach – Don Shula and Ken Blanchard

Life Is Not A Game Of Perfect – Bob Rotella

Built To Last – Jim Collins

Good To Great – Jim Collins

Acknowledgments

Since the title of my first book is *A Grander Vision - Becoming God's Leader in the Workplace*, I would like to acknowledge those who helped me learn about vision and God and leadership and writing.

My parents, Bill and Anne, who grounded me in the Christian faith through my critical formative years.

My grandfather, William Anthony Cordivari, who was the courageous immigrant, quintessential entrepreneur, businessman, leader, family man, and one of God's salt and light leaders in the workplace. His life continues as an inspiration to all of his children and grandchildren.

Cyndee, my loving wife who creates a joyful environment in which so many things become possible, like the awesome task of writing a book. And who brought my faith to the second stage and introduced me to Steve McConnell, my pastor of close to 20 years.

My children who all inspired or encouraged me to complete the book at one point or another. Thank you Bill, Jackie, Matt, Andrew, and Raquel.

My brothers and sister- Richard, Robert, Adrienne, Bruce, and Mark. You are all a treasure. Growing up with you was fun and nurturing and so much defines who I am today. Thank you.

Steve McConnell, Senior Pastor, Liberty Corner Presbyterian Church, who has likely had more cumulative influence on my spiritual development than anyone else.

Bill Hybels, whom I have only met once, but have devoured nearly everything he has written or spoken on Christian principles of leadership. And I have attended numerous leadership summits chaired by him which always leave a permanent learning mark on me.

Charles and Sandra Whitaker, my mother and father-in-law, who are such role models in the areas of faith and family. And Charles is one of God's fully devoted leaders in the workplace.

Other individuals who have made lasting imprints on my Christian faith include pastors John Galloway, Keith Brown, and Rick Dean. And my fellow brothers in Christ who carried me when I was new to the faith: Ron Peri, Jack Frost, and Barry Abell. To Jack Welch, owner of Willies Taverne, site of the 6:30AM Friday morning Bible Study which I have attended for a long time.

The people who have taught me the most about business and leadership which somehow evolved into my belief systems include: management consultant Dr. Edwin Glasscock; and leadership consultant, Dr. Stephen Payne. To Tom Ferguson, who knows more about leadership and people than just about anyone I know. My first real boss, Lou Rubinsohn, who got me excited about the world of business. The leadership role models I worked for at Johnson and Johnson who taught me so much and from each a quite different skill: Don Wemlinger, Joe Day, Ting Pau Oei, Les Riley, Larry Pickering, Tom Heyman, Eric Milledge, Peter Tattle, Gary Parlin, Jerry Ostrov, and Bernie Walsh. Through my tenure of all these bosses, Bob Wilson, Bill Weldon, and Ralph Larsen were virtually always my "big bosses." I am so grateful to God for the blessing of the total life and leadership experience at Johnson and Johnson.

Dennis Smith, President and CEO of INO Therapeutics, from whom I continue to learn advanced principles of business and leadership.

My closest former associates of many years at Ortho Derm, who were all so talented, were salt and light, and have all moved on to continuing success and their own grander visions: Jim Fay, Al Altomari, Paul Mignon, Michelle Brennan, Rosemary O'Brien, and Patty Gregory.

Harry Balser, John Haynes and Dana Hilmer read earlier versions. Thank you for your frank, helpful and constructive critiques.

Long Ridge Writers and in particular, my writing coach, Roberta Roesch, who conducts an excellent writing school and from which I have learned so much. To the editors of Writer's Digest, my monthly fix on the world of writing and publishing. Every issue is a great learning and motivational jolt on a challenging craft.

Finally and first, I give thanks to God for the gift of writing and am humbled that I might walk in the shoes of Matthew, Mark, Luke, John, Paul– the world's most important writers ever.

About the Author

Bill Cordivari grew up in the Philadelphia area. He graduated from Villanova University with a BA in Biology and received an MBA from Widener University. He worked for over two decades at Johnson and Johnson where he rose through the ranks to become President of Ortho Dermatological; a J&J business unit. Beyond his business experience, he has also held leadership positions in the military, politics, government, and local church. Bill is married with five children and currently resides in Basking Ridge, New Jersey. He gives thanks to God for the gift of writing.